simpleSTYLE

19 innovative to
traditional designs with
simple knitting techniques

simpleSTYLE

19 innovative to traditional designs with simple knitting techniques

ANN BUDD

INTERWEAVE.
interweavebooks.com

PHOTOGRAPHY: **Joe Hancock**
COVER AND INTERIOR DESIGN: **Jillfrances Gray**
TECHNICAL EDITING: **Karen Frisa**
ILLUSTRATION: **Gayle Ford**
PRODUCTION: **Katherine Jackson**

Interweave Press LLC
201 East Fourth Street
Loveland, CO 80537-5655 USA
interweavebooks.com

Printed in China by Asia Pacific Offset.

Library of Congress Cataloging-in-Publication Data

Budd, Ann, 1956-
Simple Style : 19 innovative to traditional designs with
simple knitting techniques / Ann Budd, author.
p. cm.
Includes bibliographical references and index.
ISBN 978-1-59668-062-3 (pbk.)
1. Knitted. 2. Knitting—Patterns. 3. Color in art. I. Budd,
Ann, 1956- II. Title.
TT825.A453 2008
746.43'20--dc22

2008008686

10 9 8 7 6 5 4 3 2 1

ACKNOWLEDGMENTS

Simple Style is the seventh book in the Style series, and once again, it involves the efforts of many talented people. Their creativity, enthusiasm, and hard work contribute beyond measure to the quality of each book.

For their inventive projects, thank you to designers Pam Allen, Véronik Avery, Therese Chynoweth, Kat Coyle, Cecily Glowik, Micki Hair, Alice Halbeisen, Katie Himmelberg, Margaret Hubert, Mags Kandis, Deborah Newton, Ruthie Nussbaum, Ann E. Smith, Vicki Square, and JoLene Treace. Without your dedication to knitwear design, there would be no book.

Thanks to photographer Joe Hancock for taking pictures that enhance the beauty of these knitted projects and to his assistants, John Rose and Scott Wallace, for humor and help along the way.

Thanks also to Beverly Green for help with styling; to Catherine Corona for her skillful hair and make-up artistry; Kay Osentowski and Spencer Douthit for use of their property in Fort Collins, Colorado; Prospect Homeowners Association, PNI and Linda Keseric for giving us access to Prospect, Colorado; Chautauqua Park in Boulder, Colorado; and to models Aja Dujiven, Devon McHenry, Nida Shaheen, and Jordan Shelton for looking so good.

And finally, many thanks to tech editor Karen Frisa for her meticulous pattern instructions; to copy editor Veronica Patterson for smoothing out the text; and to Jillfrances Gray, whose design for the series continues to look fresh and appealing.

CONTENTS

Knitted garments don't have to be difficult.

MAKE IT EASY

Knitting garments doesn't have to be difficult. In fact, some of the most beautiful garments are the simplest to knit. Consider the virtue of an otherwise plain sweater with an unusual edging or a well-placed band of color or texture, a simplified alternative to a complex technique. Imagine an innovative construction that minimizes seams or maximizes personal fit. These elements are the cornerstones of simplicity when it comes to knitting, and they create the beauty that unencumbered knitwear design can achieve. And the best part is that you don't have to be an expert knitter to achieve professional results.

Following the format of the other books in the popular Style series (*Scarf Style*, *Wrap Style*, *Lace Style*, *Bag Style*, *Folk Style*, and *Color Style*), *Simple Style* is a book about ways to simplify your knitting as well as a book of appealing projects designed without tedious or complicated techniques. It's not a book of remedial patterns, however. Instead, it's a collection of inventive designs from sixteen renowned knitwear designers, each of whom has mastered the challenge of designing a garment that is as simple to knit as it is simply beautiful. Each design offers an individual lesson in inspiration, technique, and, of course, style.

If you have mastered basic knitting and finishing techniques, you can knit any of the garments in this book. All it takes is a little attention to detail—consistent gauge, accurate measurements, appropriate blocking, and careful seaming. These techniques and more are explained in the Design Notebook that begins on page 106, along with helpful tips and details on how the contributing designers used basic techniques to their best advantage.

If you're concerned that you might not have the skills to tackle a full garment, don't worry. The Glossary of Techniques at the end of the book includes illustrated instructions for all the specific techniques mentioned in the projects. Along with the easy-to-follow directions and clear illustrations in the project text and Design Notebook, the Glossary of Terms and Techniques will provide all the help you need to successfully complete any project in this book.

So relax and enjoy some simple style.

simplePATTERNS

FOUR-QUARTERS PULLOVER
PAM ALLEN

Following a simple silhouette, Pam Allen worked this sweater in four easy pieces—two identical shapes and their mirror images—which she then seamed together. The center seams interrupt the natural striping tendencies of the yarn and let more of the color variation show. Pam worked the center seams on the "wrong" side so that the exposed selvedges would add a bit of textural interest. The flared shaping in the lower body is achieved by knitting upward with progressively smaller needles. There are no separate sleeves to knit—each piece is a quarter of the body and a half of a sleeve—and there are no edgings to pick up and knit. Easy!

FINISHED SIZE
About 30 (34, 38, 42, 46, 50)" (76 [86.5, 96.5, 106.5, 117, 127] cm) bust circumference. Sweater shown measures 34" (86½ cm).

YARN
Worsted weight (#4 Medium).
Shown here: LaLana Wools Forever Random Worsted Obverse (60% wool, 40% mohair; 70 yd [64 m]/57 g): yellow brick road, 6 (7, 8, 9, 10, 10) skeins.

NEEDLES
Sizes U.S. 8, 9, 10, 10½, and 11 (5, 5.5, 6, 6.5, and 8 mm). Adjust needle size if necessary to obtain the correct gauge.

NOTIONS
Removable markers; tapestry needle.

GAUGE
16 stitches and 23 rows = 4" (10 cm) in stockinette stitch on smallest needles.

NOTES

✛ The front and back are each made in two separate panels that are sewn together.

✛ At the center front or back edge of each piece and at the sleeve cuffs, knit the two edge stitches on every row. The center seams are worked on the right side, so it's important that the edges are tidy. If preferred, the sleeve cuffs could be worked in stockinette stitch for a more casual look.

✛ The neckline shaping is worked on both right- and wrong-side rows for a smooth edge.

✛ Because of the large stitch gauge and extra seams, selvedge stitches are included in schematic measurements, but not in the finished size.

LEFT FRONT

With largest needles and using the long-tail method (see Glossary), CO 32 (36, 40, 44, 48, 52) sts. Knit 3 rows. *Next row:* (WS) K2, purl to end. Change to St st (knit RS rows; purl WS rows), keeping 2 sts at center front in garter st (see Notes), and work even until piece measures 2½" (6.5 cm) from CO. Change to size 10½ (6.5 mm) needles and cont in patt until piece measures 5" (12.5 cm) from CO. Change to size 10 (6 mm) needles and cont in patt until piece measures 7½" (19 cm) from CO. Change to size 9 (5.5 mm) needles and cont in patt until piece measures 10" (25.5 cm) from CO. Change to size 8 (5 mm) needles and cont in patt until piece measures 13½ (13½, 14, 15, 15, 15)" (34.5 [34.5, 35.5, 38, 38, 38] cm) from CO, ending with a WS row. Place removable marker on this row to mark beg of sleeve shaping (work the same number of rows to the sleeve shaping on the other pieces).

Shape Sleeve

Inc row: (RS) K2, M1 (see Glossary), work to end—1 st inc'd. Work 3 rows even. Rep inc row—34 (38, 42, 46, 50, 54) sts. Work 1 row even. Using the knitted method (see Glossary), CO 2 sts at the beg of the next 4 RS rows, then CO 3 sts at the beg of the next 2 RS rows, then CO 10 sts at beg of next RS row, then CO 10 (12, 14, 15, 15, 15) sts at beg of next RS row, then CO 23 (29, 31, 34, 38, 38) sts at beg of next RS row—91 (103, 111, 119, 127, 131) sts total. Keeping 2 sts at cuff edge in garter st (see Notes), work even in patt until piece measures 6" (15 cm) from sleeve marker, ending with a RS row.

Shape Neck

Next row: (WS) BO 4 (5, 5, 6, 6, 7) sts, work to end—87 (98, 106, 113, 121, 124) sts rem. Cont to shape neck edge every row as foll: *Next row:* (RS) Knit to last 2 sts, k2tog—86 (97, 105, 112, 120, 123) sts rem. *Next row:* (WS) Slipping the first st of the row, BO 2 sts, work

A visible seam allowance makes a nice design element.

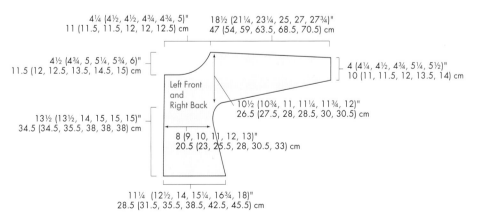

4¼ (4½, 4½, 4¾, 4¾, 5)"
11 (11.5, 11.5, 12, 12, 12.5) cm

18½ (21¼, 23¼, 25, 27, 27¾)"
47 (54, 59, 63.5, 68.5, 70.5) cm

4½ (4¾, 5, 5¼, 5¾, 6)"
11.5 (12, 12.5, 13.5, 14.5, 15) cm

4 (4¼, 4½, 4¾, 5¼, 5½)"
10 (11, 11.5, 12, 13.5, 14) cm

Left Front and Right Back

10½ (10¾, 11, 11¼, 11¾, 12)"
26.5 (27.5, 28, 28.5, 30, 30.5) cm

13½ (13½, 14, 15, 15, 15)"
34.5 (34.5, 35.5, 38, 38, 38) cm

8 (9, 10, 11, 12, 13)"
20.5 (23, 25.5, 28, 30.5, 33) cm

11¼ (12½, 14, 15¼, 16¾, 18)"
28.5 (31.5, 35.5, 38.5, 42.5, 45.5) cm

to end—84 (95, 103, 110, 118, 121) sts rem. *Next row:* Knit to last 2 sts, k2tog—1 st dec'd. *Next row:* P2tog, purl to last 2 sts, k2—1 st dec'd. Rep last 2 rows 2 more times, then dec 1 st at neck edge every RS row 4 times and *at the same time* when cuff of sleeve measures 4 (4¼, 4½, 4¾, 5¼, 5½)" (10 [11, 11.5, 12, 13.5, 14] cm), BO 11 (12, 13, 14, 15, 16) sts at cuff edge (beg of RS rows) 6 times—8 (13, 15, 16, 18, 15) sts rem. BO all sts.

RIGHT FRONT

With largest needles and using the long-tail method, CO 32 (36, 40, 44, 48, 52) sts. Knit 3 rows. *Next row:* (WS) Purl to last 2 sts, k2. Change to St st, keeping 2 sts at center front in garter st (see Notes), and work even until piece measures 2½" (6.5 cm) from CO. Change to size 10½ (6.5 mm) needles and cont in patt until piece measures 5" (12.5 cm) from CO. Change to size 10 (6 mm) needles and cont in patt until piece measures 7½" (19 cm) from CO. Change to size 9 (5.5 mm) needles and cont in patt until piece measures 10" (25.5 cm) from CO. Change to size 8 (5 mm) needles and cont in patt until piece measures 13½ (13½, 14, 15, 15, 15)" (34.5 [34.5, 35.5, 38, 38, 38] cm) from CO, ending with a WS row. Place removable marker on this row to mark beg of sleeve shaping.

Shape Sleeve

Inc row: (RS) Knit to last 2 sts, M1, k2—1 st inc'd. Work 3 rows even. Rep inc row—34 (38, 42, 46, 50, 54) sts. Using the knitted method, CO 2 sts at the beg of the next 4 WS rows, then CO 3 sts at the beg of the next 2 WS rows, then CO 10 sts at beg of next WS row, then CO 10 (12, 14, 15, 15, 15) sts at beg of next WS row, then CO 23 (29, 31, 34, 38, 38) sts at beg of next WS row—91 (103, 111, 119, 127, 131) sts total. Keeping 2 sts at cuff edge in garter st, work even in patt until piece measures 6" (15 cm) from sleeve marker, ending with a WS row.

Work the sleeves together with the front and back to eliminate armhole seams.

Shape Neck

Next row: (RS) BO 4 (5, 5, 6, 6, 7) sts, knit to end—87 (98, 106, 113, 121, 124) sts rem. Cont to shape neck edge every row as foll: *Next row:* (WS) K2, purl to last 2 sts, p2togtbl (see Glossary)—86 (97, 105, 112, 120, 123) sts rem. *Next row:* Slipping the first st of the row, BO 2 sts, knit to end—84 (95, 103, 110, 118, 121) sts rem. *Next row:* K2, purl to last 2 sts, p2togtbl—1 st dec'd. *Next row:* Ssk (see Glossary), knit to end—1 st dec'd. Rep the last 2 rows 2 more times, then dec 1 st at neck edge every RS row 4 times and *at the same time* when cuff of sleeve measures 4 (4¼, 4½, 4¾, 5¼, 5½)" (10 [11, 11.5, 12, 13.5, 14] cm), BO 11 (12, 13, 14, 15, 16) sts at cuff edge (beg of WS rows) 6 times—8 (13, 15, 16, 18, 15) sts rem. BO all sts.

LEFT BACK

Work as for right front.

RIGHT BACK

Work as for left front.

FINISHING

Weave in loose ends. Steam pieces well. With yarn threaded on a tapestry needle, WS facing, and using the mattress st (see Glossary), sew center front and center back seams. Sew shoulder and upper sleeve seams. Sew side and sleeve seams. Press seams flat.

Cecily Glowik designed this sweater with a low, broad neckline that fits beautifully whether you wear the sweater with the buttons in front or back. The body is worked in the round to the armholes, the sleeves are added, then the yoke is worked in a single piece to the wide neck opening. The yoke is shaped with decreases that are cleverly disguised in ribs that taper from larger repeats at the base to smaller repeats at the neck. Wide ribs at the hem extend partway up the sides to give a hint of waist shaping. Stitches for the button and buttonhole bands are picked up and knitted along the front opening. Knitted in 100% cashmere, this sweater is pure luxury.

LOWER BODY

With larger needle, CO 148 (164, 188, 220) sts. Do not join. *Set-up rib:* (WS) P4 (4, 0, 0), *k4, p4; rep from * to last 0 (0, 4, 4) sts, k0 (0, 4, 4). Work in patt as established (knit the knits and purl the purls) until piece measures 2" (5 cm) from CO, ending with a WS row. *Next row:* (RS) K24 (32, 36, 44), [p4, k4] 3 times, k16 (16, 24, 32), [p4, k4] 3 times, k16 (16, 24, 32), [p4, k4] 3 times, k20 (28, 32, 40). Work in patt as established until piece measures 4" (10 cm) from CO, ending with a WS row. *Next row:* (RS) K32 (40, 44, 52), p4, k36 (36, 44, 52), p4, k36 (36, 44, 52), p4, knit to end. Work in patt as established until piece measures 6" (15 cm) from CO, ending with a WS row. Change to St st and work even until piece measures 13 (13, 12, 11)" (33 [33, 30.5, 28] cm) from CO, ending with a WS row.

Divide for Fronts and Back

(RS) K32 (36, 40, 48) for right front, BO next 8 (8, 12, 12) sts for right armhole, k68 (76, 84, 100) for back, BO next 8 (8, 12, 12) sts for left armhole, k32 (36, 40, 48) for left front. Place sts on holders or waste yarn and set aside.

FINISHED SIZE
About 33 (36½, 41¾, 49)" (84 [92.5, 106, 124.5] cm) bust circumference, buttoned. Sweater shown measures 33" (84 cm).

YARN
Worsted weight (#4 Medium).
Shown here: Classic Elite Stormy (100% cashmere; 110 yd [101 m]/50 g): #10369 rust, 7 (8, 8, 9) skeins.

NEEDLES
Body and sleeves—size U.S. 8 (5 mm): 32" (80 cm) circular (cir). Edging—size U.S. 7 (4.5 mm): 24" (60 cm) cir. Adjust needle size if necessary to obtain the correct gauge.

NOTIONS
Stitch holders or waste yarn; tapestry needle; sixteen ½" (1.3 cm) buttons.

GAUGE
18 stitches and 26 rows = 4" (10 cm) in stockinette stitch on larger needle.

Hide decreases
in rib stitches.

SLEEVES

With larger needle, CO 38 (38, 42, 42) sts. Do not join. *Set-up rib:* (RS) K1 (1, 3, 3), p0 (0, 4, 4), *k4, p4; rep from * to last 5 (5, 3, 3) sts, k5 (5, 3, 3). Work in patt as established until piece measures 2" (5 cm) from CO, ending with a WS row. Change to St st. *Inc row:* (RS) K2, LLI (see Glossary), knit to last 2 sts, RLI (see Glossary), k2—2 sts inc'd. Inc 1 st each end of needle in this manner every 8 (8, 8, 6) rows 10 (12, 12, 14) more times—60 (64, 68, 72) sts. Work even until piece measures 18" (45.5 cm) from CO, ending with a WS row. BO 4 (4, 6, 6) sts at beg of next 2 rows—52 (56, 56, 60) sts rem.

YOKE

Rejoin yarn to WS of left front and with larger needle join pieces as foll: P32 (36, 40, 48) left front sts, p52 (56, 56, 60) left sleeve sts, p68 (76, 84, 100) back sts, p52 (56, 56, 60) right sleeve sts, p32 (36, 40, 48) right front sts—236 (260, 276, 316) sts total. Work 2 rows in St st, then work in St st for 0 (0, 1, 2)" (0 [0, 2.5, 5] cm) more, ending with a WS row. *Next row:* (RS) *K4, p4; rep from * to last 4 sts, k4. Work in patt as established until rib section measures 2" (5 cm), ending with a WS row. *Next row:* (RS) K4, p4, *k1, k2tog, k1, p4; rep from * to last 4 sts, k4—208 (229, 243, 278) sts rem. Work even as established until rib section measures 3" (7.5 cm), ending with a WS row.

Sizes 33 (36½)" only

Next row: (RS) K4, p1, p2tog, p1, *k3, p1, p2tog, p1; rep from * to last 4 sts, k4—179 (197) sts rem. Work in patt as established until rib section measures 4" (10 cm), ending with a WS row. *Next row:* (RS) K4, p3, *sl 1, k2tog, psso, p3; rep from * to last 4 sts, k4—123 (135) sts rem.

Size 41¾" only

Next row: (RS) K4, p1, p2tog, p1, [k3, (p2tog) twice, k3, p1, p2tog, p1] 8 times, [k3, p1, p2tog, p1, k3, (p2tog) twice] 8 times, k3, p1, p2tog, p1, k4—193 sts rem. Work in patt as

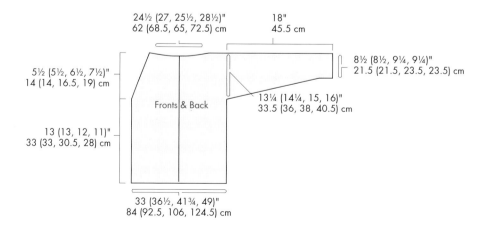

24½ (27, 25½, 28½)"
62 (68.5, 65, 72.5) cm

18"
45.5 cm

5½ (5½, 6½, 7½)"
14 (14, 16.5, 19) cm

8½ (8½, 9¼, 9¼)"
21.5 (21.5, 23.5, 23.5) cm

Fronts & Back

13¼ (14¼, 15, 16)"
33.5 (36, 38, 40.5) cm

13 (13, 12, 11)"
33 (33, 30.5, 28) cm

33 (36½, 41¾, 49)"
84 (92.5, 106, 124.5) cm

established until rib section measures 4" (10 cm), ending with a WS row. *Next row:* (RS) K4, p3, [sl 1, k2tog, psso, p2, sl 1, k2tog, psso, p3] 8 times, [sl 1, k2tog, psso, p3, sl 1, k2tog, psso, p2] 8 times, sl 1, k2tog, psso, p3, k4—127 sts rem.

Size 49" only

Next row: (RS) K4, [p2tog] twice, *k3, p1, p2tog, p1, k3, [p2tog] twice; rep from * to last 4 sts, k4—219 sts rem. Work in patt as established until rib section measures 4" (10 cm), ending with a WS row. *Next row:* (RS) K4, p2, *sl 1, k2tog, psso, p3, sl 1, k2tog, psso, p2; rep from * to last 4 sts, k4—143 sts rem.

Neckband

All sizes

Change to smaller needle. Work 3 rows even. *Next row:* (RS) K4, p1, *k1, p1; rep from * to last 4 sts, k4. Work in patt as established for ½" (1.3 cm), ending with a WS row. With RS facing, BO all sts kwise.

FINISHING

Block piece to measurements. Weave in loose ends. With yarn threaded on a tapestry needle, sew underarm seams. Sew sleeve seams.

Buttonhole Band

With smaller needle and RS facing, pick up and knit 80 sts evenly spaced along right front edge. Work back and forth in rows as foll:

Row 1: (WS) *K5, p5; rep from *.

Row 2: (RS; buttonhole row) *K2, yo, k2tog, k1, p2, yo, p2tog, p1; rep from *.

Work 1 row even as established. With RS facing, BO all sts kwise.

Buttonband

With smaller needle and RS facing, pick up and knit 80 sts evenly spaced along left front edge. *Set-up row:* (WS) *P5, k5; rep from *. Work 2 more rows in rib as established. With RS facing, BO all sts kwise.

With yarn threaded on a tapestry needle, sew buttons to left front opposite buttonholes.

Wear the buttons
in the front or back!

For this modern take on the traditional Henley pullover, Micki Hair chose organic cotton yarn in three natural colors. She worked the body in stockinette stitch and added narrow bands of contrasting ribbing to control the amount of roll along the cast-on and bind-off edges. To eliminate side and sleeve seams, Micki worked most of the body in the round. She picked up stitches for the sleeves at the armholes and worked the sleeves in the round to the cuffs. Paired decreases and increases at the side "seams" provide subtle waist shaping. A bit of playful embroidery and crocheted ties at the neck add a polished finish to the pullover.

BODY

With MC and longer cir needle, CO 190 (200, 210, 220) sts. Place marker (pm) and join for working in rnds, being careful not to twist sts. Knit 6 rnds. With CC1, knit 1 rnd, then work 2 rnds in k1, p1 rib. Change to MC. K95 (100, 105, 110), pm for side "seam," knit to end of rnd—95 (100, 105, 110) sts each for front and back. Work even until piece measures 3 (3, 3¼, 3½)" (7.5 [7.5, 8.5, 9] cm) from top of rib. *Dec rnd:* *K2tog, knit to 2 sts before m, ssk (see Glossary), slip marker (sl m); rep from *—4 sts dec'd. Work 5 (6, 7, 8) rnds even. Rep the last 6 (7, 8, 9) rnds 2 more times—178 (188, 198, 208) sts rem. Work even until piece measures 6½ (7, 7¾, 8½)" (16.5 [18, 19.5, 21.5] cm) from top of rib. *Inc rnd:* *K1, LLI (see Glossary), work to 1 st before m, RLI (see Glossary), k1, sl m; rep from *—4 sts inc'd. Work 5 (6, 7, 8) rnds even. Rep the last 6 (7, 8, 9) rnds 2 more times—190 (200, 210, 220) sts. Work even until piece measures 12 (13½, 14, 14½)" (30.5 [34.5, 35.5, 37] cm) from top of rib.

DIVIDE FOR FRONT AND BACK

K95 (100, 105, 110) and place these sts on holder for front, knit to end—95 (100, 105, 110) back sts.

BACK

Work 95 (100, 105, 110) back sts back and forth in rows until armholes measure 8 (8½, 9, 9½)" (20.5 [21.5, 23, 24] cm), ending with a WS row.

FINISHED SIZE

About 36¼ (38, 40, 42)" (92 [96.5, 101.5, 106.5] cm) bust circumference. Sweater shown measures 36¼" (92 cm).

YARN

Worsted weight (#4 Medium).

Shown here: Lion Brand Yarn Lion Organic Cotton (100% cotton; 82 yd [75 m]/50 g): #003 bark (brown; MC), 12 (14, 15, 16) balls; #002 almond (off-white; CC1) and #004 cypress (sage green; CC2), 1 ball each (all sizes).

NEEDLES

Size U.S. 8 (5 mm): 16" and 24" (40 and 60 cm) circular (cir) and set of 4 or 5 double-pointed (dpn). Adjust needle size if necessary to obtain the correct gauge.

NOTIONS

Markers (m); stitch holders; tapestry needle; size E/4 (3.5 mm) crochet hook.

GAUGE

21 stitches and 28 rounds = 4" (10 cm) in stockinette stitch worked in rounds.

Shape Shoulders and Neck

Shape shoulders with short-rows (see Glossary) as foll: (RS) K30 (32, 34, 36), place next 35 (36, 37, 38) sts on holder for back neck, place rem 30 (32, 34, 36) sts on another holder to work later for left shoulder. Turn work, p20 (20, 22, 24), wrap next st, turn work, k20 (20, 22, 24), turn work, p10 (10, 10, 12), wrap next st, turn work, k10 (10, 10, 12). Place these 30 (32, 34, 36) sts on a holder for right shoulder. With RS facing, rejoin yarn to 30 (32, 34, 36) left shoulder sts and work short-rows as foll: K20 (20, 22, 24), wrap next st, turn work, p20 (20, 22, 24), turn work, k10 (10, 10, 12), wrap next st, turn work, p10 (10, 10, 12). Place sts on holder.

FRONT

Return 95 (100, 105, 110) front sts to longer cir needle and work even in St st until armholes measure 4 (4½, 4½, 4½)" (10 [11.5, 11.5, 11.5] cm), ending with a WS row.

Shape Neck

(RS) K46 (48, 51, 53), BO center 3 (4, 3, 4) sts, knit to end of row—46 (48, 51, 53) sts rem each side. Working each side separately, work even until piece measures 2½ (2½, 2¾, 3)" (6.5

Add a bit of embroidery to liven up a simple design.

[6.5, 7, 7.5] cm) from center BO. At each neck edge, BO 5 (5, 6, 6) sts once, then BO 4 sts 2 times, then BO 3 sts once—30 (32, 34, 36) sts rem each side. Work even until armholes measure 8 (8½, 9, 9½)" (20.5 [21.5, 23, 24] cm).

Shape Shoulders

Shape shoulders as for back.

JOIN FRONT TO BACK AT SHOULDERS

Place the 30 (32, 34, 36) held left front shoulder sts on dpn and corresponding 30 (32, 34, 36) back shoulder sts on another dpn. Hold pieces with RS facing tog and use the three-needle method (see Glossary) to BO the sts tog. Rep for right shoulder.

SLEEVES

With MC, shorter cir needle, RS facing, and beg at base of armhole, pick up and knit 94 (100, 106, 112) sts evenly spaced around armhole. Pm and join for working in rnds. Work 5 (4, 4, 4) rnds even. *Dec rnd:* K2tog, knit to last 2 sts, ssk—2 sts dec'd. Changing to dpn when necessary, rep dec rnd every 4th rnd 0 (4, 15, 17) more times, then every 5th rnd 23 (21, 12, 12) times—46 (48, 50, 52) sts rem. Work 5 (3, 5, 0) rnds even. With CC1, knit 1 rnd, then work 2 rnds in k1, p1 rib. With MC, knit 6 rnds. BO all sts kwise.

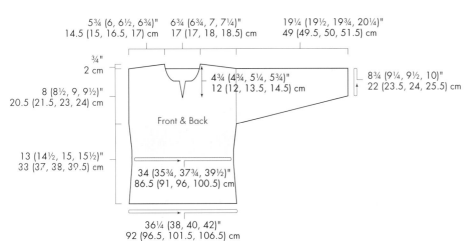

5¾ (6, 6½, 6¾)"
14.5 (15, 16.5, 17) cm

6¾ (6¾, 7, 7¼)"
17 (17, 18, 18.5) cm

19¼ (19½, 19¾, 20¼)"
49 (49.5, 50, 51.5) cm

¾"
2 cm

4¾ (4¾, 5¼, 5¾)"
12 (12, 13.5, 14.5) cm

8¾ (9¼, 9½, 10)"
22 (23.5, 24, 25.5) cm

8 (8½, 9, 9½)"
20.5 (21.5, 23, 24) cm

Front & Back

13 (14½, 15, 15½)"
33 (37, 38, 39.5) cm

34 (35¾, 37¾, 39½)"
86.5 (91, 96, 100.5) cm

36¼ (38, 40, 42)"
92 (96.5, 101.5, 106.5) cm

Pick up stitches at the armholes and work the sleeves downward to the cuffs.

FINISHING

Weave in loose ends.

Neckband

With CC1, cir needle, RS facing, and beg at right shoulder, pick up and knit 4 sts to holder, k35 (36, 37, 38) back neck sts from holder, then pick up and knit 4 sts to left shoulder, 45 (47, 50, 52) sts to center front BO sts, 1 st in each of next 3 (4, 3, 4) BO sts, and 45 (47, 50, 52) sts to right shoulder—136 (142, 148, 154) sts total. Pm and join for working in rnds. Work in k1, p1 rib for 2 rnds. Change to MC and knit 6 rnds. BO all sts kwise.

Ties (make 2)

With crochet hook, make a chain (see Glossary) about 8" (20.5 cm) long. Fasten off. Sew one tie to each front at top of slit.

Embroidery

With CC1 threaded on a tapestry needle, work modified cross sts as shown in photographs, evenly spaced around neck and lower body edges, working the large X across 3 sts and 4 rows and the small X over 1 st and 2 rows. Work three modified cross sts at each wrist. With CC2 threaded on a tapestry needle, work 4 French knots (see Glossary) around each modified cross.

Lay sweater flat with front side facing up. Spritz lightly with water, then steam with a hot iron thoroughly. Allow to air-dry thoroughly. Rep for other side. Steam-block shoulder seams.

Kazumi, a Japanese term for harmonious beauty, is an essential quality of good Japanese design, in which each element is used to its best effect. JoLene Treace relied on this principle when designing her ribbed pullover. She began with a decorative cast-on, followed by straight ribs dotted with a delicate eyelet pattern at the hem and cuffs. Overall, the pattern reminds JoLene of the contrast between delicate cherry blossoms and the stark and angular twigs of cherry trees before the leaves appear. JoLene added decreases and increases at the side seams to shape the waist and enhance the feminine look, and she finished the neck with a knit-two-purl-two ribbing that maintains the integrity of the ribs at the center front and back.

NOTES

✤ A selvedge stitch is worked at each edge of each piece to facilitate seaming. Knit the selvedge stitches on right-side rows and purl them on wrong-side rows.

✤ Work decreases adjacent to the selvedge stitches; do not include the selvedge stitches in the decreases.

FINISHED SIZE

About 36½ (41, 45, 48½, 52½)" (92.5 [104, 114.5, 123, 133.5] cm) bust circumference. Sweater shown measures 36½" (92.5 cm).

YARN

DK weight (#3 Light).

Shown here: Sirdar Snuggly Baby Bamboo (80% bamboo; 20% wool; 105 yd [96 m]/50 g): #132 putty, 12 (14, 15, 16, 18) balls.

NEEDLES

Body and sleeves—size U.S. 3 (3.25 mm): straight and 16" (40 cm) circular (cir). Neckband—size U.S. 2 (2.75 mm): 16" (40 cm) cir. Adjust needle size if necessary to obtain the correct gauge.

NOTIONS

Stitch holders; marker (m); tapestry needle.

GAUGE

26 stitches and 34 rows = 4" (10 cm) in rib pattern on larger needles, blocked with moderate stretch.

BACK

With larger straight needles and using the Channel Island method (see Glossary), CO 126 (138, 150, 166, 178) sts. Working the first and last st of each row in St st for selvedge sts (see Notes) throughout, purl 1 (WS) row. Beg and end as indicated for your size, work center 124 (136, 148, 164, 176) sts according to Rows 1–6 of Kazumi chart. *Dec row:* (RS; chart row 7) K1 (selvedge st), k2tog, work in patt to last 3 sts, ssk (see Glossary), k1 (selvedge st)—2 sts dec'd. Work 3 rows even in patt. Rep the shaping of the last 4 rows 4 (6, 6, 8, 8) more times, cont in k2, p2 rib as established after Row 26 of chart—116 (124, 136, 148, 160) sts rem. Rep dec row every RS row 9 (5, 5, 1, 1) time(s)—98 (114, 126, 146, 158) sts rem. Work even for 8 rows. *Inc row:* (RS) K1 (selvedge st), M1L (see Glossary), work in rib as established to last st, M1R (see Glossary), k1 (selvedge st)—2 sts inc'd. Work 3 (3, 3, 5, 5) rows even. Rep the last 4 (4, 4, 6, 6) rows 8 (8, 8, 4, 4) more times, then rep inc row once more—118 (134, 146, 158, 170) sts. Work even in rib until piece measures 14" (35.5 cm) from CO, ending with a WS row.

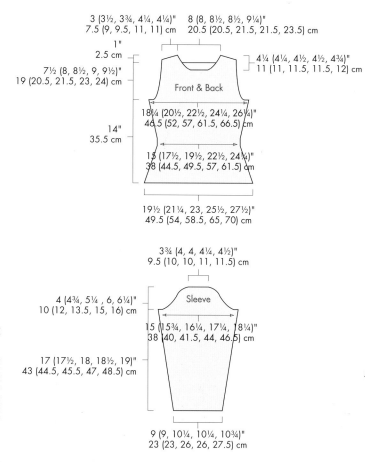

3 (3½, 3¾, 4¼, 4¼)"
7.5 (9, 9.5, 11, 11) cm

8 (8, 8½, 8½, 9¼)"
20.5 (20.5, 21.5, 21.5, 23.5) cm

1"
2.5 cm

7½ (8, 8½, 9, 9½)"
19 (20.5, 21.5, 23, 24) cm

4¼ (4¼, 4½, 4½, 4¾)"
11 (11, 11.5, 11.5, 12) cm

Front & Back

18¼ (20½, 22½, 24¼, 26¼)"
46.5 (52, 57, 61.5, 66.5) cm

14"
35.5 cm

15 (17½, 19½, 22½, 24¼)"
38 (44.5, 49.5, 57, 61.5) cm

19½ (21¼, 23, 25½, 27½)"
49.5 (54, 58.5, 65, 70) cm

3¾ (4, 4, 4¼, 4½)"
9.5 (10, 10, 11, 11.5) cm

4 (4¾, 5¼ , 6, 6¼)"
10 (12, 13.5, 15, 16) cm

Sleeve

15 (15¾, 16¼, 17¼, 18¼)"
38 (40, 41.5, 44, 46.5) cm

17 (17½, 18, 18½, 19)"
43 (44.5, 45.5, 47, 48.5) cm

9 (9, 10¼, 10¼, 10¾)"
23 (23, 26, 26, 27.5) cm

Kazumi

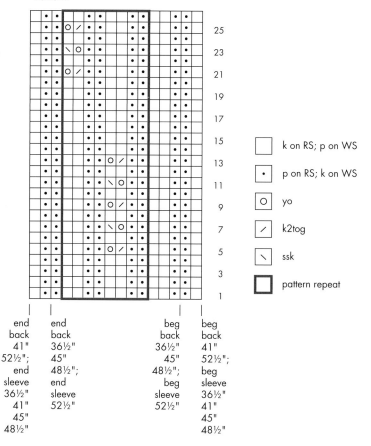

	k on RS; p on WS
•	p on RS; k on WS
O	yo
/	k2tog
\	ssk
	pattern repeat

end back 41" 52½"; end sleeve 36½" 41" 45" 48½"

end back 36½" 45" 48½"; end sleeve 52½"

beg back 36½" 45" 48½"; beg sleeve 52½"

beg back 41" 52½"; beg sleeve 36½" 41" 45" 48½"

Shape Armholes

BO 5 (6, 7, 8, 9) sts at beg of next 2 rows, then BO 2 sts at beg of foll 6 (6, 8, 10, 12) rows—96 (110, 116, 122, 128) sts rem. Dec 1 st each end of needle every RS row 3 (6, 6, 6, 6) times—90 (98, 104, 110, 116) sts rem. Work even in rib until armholes measure 6 (6½, 7, 7½, 8)" (15 [16.5, 18, 19, 20.5] cm), ending with a WS row.

Shape Neck

(RS) Keeping in rib, work 28 (32, 33, 36, 37) sts, place next 34 (34, 38, 38, 42) sts on holder for back neck, join a second ball of yarn, work to end—28 (32, 33, 36, 37) sts each side. Working each side separately and working the first and last st of each section as selvedge sts, cont in rib and *at the same time* at each neck edge BO 3 sts once, then BO 2 sts 2 times—21 (25, 26, 29, 30) sts rem each side. Dec 1 st at each neck edge every RS row 2 times—19 (23, 24, 27, 28) sts rem each side—armholes measure 7½ (8, 8½, 9, 9½)" (19 [20.5, 21.5, 23, 24] cm).

Shape Shoulders

At each armhole edge, BO 5 (6, 6, 7, 7) sts 3 times, then BO rem 4 (5, 6, 6, 7) sts.

FRONT

CO and work as for back until armholes measure 4¼ (4¾, 5, 5½, 5¾)" (11 [12, 12.5, 14, 14.5] cm), ending with a WS row.

Shape Neck

(RS) Work 36 (40, 43, 46, 48) sts, place next 18 (18, 18, 18, 20) sts on holder for front neck, join second ball of yarn, and work to end—36 (40, 43, 46, 48) sts rem each side. Working each side separately and working the first and last st as selvedge sts, cont in rib and *at the same time* at each neck

Consider the merits of a
decorative cast-on.

Sometimes, a little bit of
lace is just enough!

edge, BO 2 sts 5 (5, 6, 6, 6) times—26 (30, 31, 34, 36) sts rem each side. Dec 1 st at each neck edge every RS row 7 (7, 7, 7, 8) times—19 (23, 24, 27, 28) sts rem each side. Work even in rib until armholes measure same as back to beg of shoulder shaping.

Shape Shoulders

Shape shoulders as for back.

SLEEVES

With larger straight needles and using the Channel Island method, CO 58 (58, 66, 66, 70) sts. Working the first and last st as selvedge sts throughout, purl 1 row. Beg and end as indicated for your size, work center 56 (56, 64, 64, 68) sts according to Rows 1–26 of Kazumi chart, then cont in rib as established and *at the same time* inc 1 st each end of needle every 6 (4, 6, 6, 4)th row 17 (1, 13, 23, 1) time(s), then every 8 (6, 8, 0, 6)th row 3 (21, 7, 0, 23) times—98 (102, 106, 112, 118) sts. Work even in rib until piece measures 17 (17½, 18, 18½, 19)" (43 [44.5, 45.5, 47, 48.5] cm) from CO, ending with a WS row.

Shape Cap

Keeping in patt, BO 5 (6, 7, 8, 9) sts at beg of next 2 rows, then BO 3 sts at beg of foll 4 (2, 2, 2, 2) rows, then BO 2 sts at beg of foll 8 (6, 8, 4, 2) rows—60 (72, 70, 82, 90) sts rem. Dec 1 st each end of needle every RS row 4 (9, 12, 17, 19) times—52 (54, 46, 48, 52) sts rem. BO 2 sts at beg of next 8 (8, 4, 4, 8) rows, then BO 3 sts at beg of foll 4 (4, 4, 4, 2) rows—24 (26, 26, 28, 30) sts rem. BO all sts.

FINISHING

Block pieces to measurements. Weave in loose ends.

Seams

With yarn threaded on a tapestry needle, sew front to back at shoulders. Sew sleeve caps into armholes, matching centers of sleeves with shoulder seams. Sew sleeve and side seams.

Neckband

With larger cir needle, RS facing, and beg at left shoulder seam, pick up and knit 28 (28, 30, 30, 31) sts along left neck edge, work 18 (18, 18, 18, 20) held front neck sts in patt as established, pick up and knit 28 (28, 30, 30, 31) sts along right neck edge to shoulder seam and 14 sts along right back neck, work 34 (34, 38, 38, 42) held back neck sts in patt as established, then pick up and knit 14 sts along left back neck—136 (136, 144, 144, 152) sts total. Place marker (pm) and join for working in rnds. Maintaining rib as established at center front and back and beg with k2 (k2, p2, p2, k2), work in k2, p2 rib for 4 rnds. Change to smaller cir needle and work 4 rnds more. BO all sts in patt.

Block again if desired.

If you've ever shied away from knitting cardigans because you don't like to fuss with buttons and buttonbands, take a lesson from Margaret Hubert. Inspired by a jacket on display in a trendy Italian clothing shop, Margaret worked a single buttonhole at the neck edge of the right front to accommodate the single-button closure. To simplify the knitting, she worked each piece in stockinette stitch and allowed the edges to curl naturally. Other than the collar, there are no stitches to pick up, and there is no buttonhole spacing to calculate. Margaret worked full-fashioned decreases at the armholes and added a classic foldover collar. At fewer than four stitches per inch, this jacket knits up in no time!

NOTES

✦ This sweater is worked entirely in stockinette stitch so that the edges intentionally curl to form the edging.

BACK

With smaller needles, CO 70 (74, 78) sts. Work even in St st (knit RS rows; purl WS rows) until piece measures 11½ (12, 12½)" (29 [30.5, 31.5] cm) from CO, ending with a WS row.

Shape Armholes

BO 3 sts at beg of next 2 rows—64 (68, 72) sts rem. *Dec row:* (RS) K2, ssk (see Glossary), knit to last 4 sts, k2tog, k2—2 sts dec'd. Dec 1 st each end of needle in this manner every RS row 5 more times—52 (56, 60) sts rem. Work even until armholes measure 7½ (8, 8½)" (19 [20.5, 21.5] cm), ending with a WS row.

Shape Shoulders

BO 15 (16, 17) sts at beg of next 2 rows—22 (24, 26) sts rem. Place sts on holder.

FINISHED SIZE
About 37½ (39½, 41½)" (95 [100.5, 105.5] cm) bust circumference. Sweater shown measures 39½" (100.5 cm).

YARN
Worsted weight (#4 Medium).

Shown here: Fiesta Yarns Kokopelli (60% brushed kid mohair, 40% wool; 125 yd [114 m]/113 g): #K14 squash blossom, 6 (7, 7) skeins.

NEEDLES
Body and sleeves—size U.S. 10 (6 mm). Collar edging—size U.S. 10½ (6.5 mm). Adjust needle size if necessary to obtain the correct gauge.

NOTIONS
Stitch holder; tapestry needle; one 1¾" (4.5 cm) button (button shown is from Dill Buttons of America).

GAUGE
15 stitches and 18 rows = 4" (10 cm) in stockinette stitch on smaller needles.

LEFT FRONT

With smaller needles, CO 39 (41, 43) sts. Work even in St st until piece measures same as back to armholes, ending with a WS row.

Shape Armhole

(RS) BO 3 sts, knit to end—36 (38, 40) sts rem. Purl 1 WS row. *Dec row:* (RS) K2, ssk, knit to end—1 st dec'd. Dec 1 st at armhole edge in this manner every RS row 5 more times—30 (32, 34) sts rem. Work even until armhole measures 5½ (6, 6½)" (14 [15, 16.5] cm), ending with a RS row.

Shape Neck

(WS) BO 9 (10, 11) sts, purl to end—21 (22, 23) sts rem. Dec 1 st (k2tog on RS rows; p2tog on WS rows) at neck edge every row 6 times—15 (16, 17) sts rem. Work even until armhole measures 7½ (8, 8½)" (19 [20.5, 21.5] cm), ending with a WS row. BO all sts.

RIGHT FRONT

With smaller needles, CO and work as for left front to beg of armhole shaping, ending with a RS row.

Shape Armhole

(WS) BO 3 sts, purl to end—36 (38, 40) sts rem. *Dec row:* (RS) Knit to last 4 sts, k2tog, k2—1 st dec'd. Dec 1 st at armhole edge in this manner every RS row 5 more times—30 (32, 34) sts rem. Work even until armhole measures 4½ (5, 5½)" (11.5 [12.5, 14] cm), ending with a WS row. *Buttonhole row:* (RS) K2, BO 4 sts, knit to end. *Next row:* (WS) Purl to gap formed by BO sts in previous row, use the backward-loop method (see Glossary) to CO 4 sts over gap, p2—buttonhole completed. Knit 1 row. Purl 1 row.

Shape Neck

(RS) BO 9 (10, 11) sts, knit to end—21 (22, 23) sts rem. Dec 1 st (k2tog on RS rows; p2tog on WS rows) at neck edge every row 6 times—15 (16, 17) sts rem. Work even until armhole measures 7½ (8, 8½)" (19 [20.5, 21.5] cm), ending with a RS row. BO all sts.

SLEEVES

With smaller needles, CO 41 (45, 45) sts. Work in St st until piece measures 2 (3, 3)" (5 [7.5, 7.5] cm) from CO, ending with a WS row. *Inc row:* (RS) K1, M1 (see Glossary), knit to last st, M1, k1—2 sts inc'd. Inc 1 st each end of needle in this manner every 14 (14, 12)th row 4 (4, 5) more times—51 (55, 57) sts. Work even until piece measures 16 (16½, 17)" (40.5 [42, 43] cm) from CO, ending with a WS row.

Shape Cap

BO 3 sts at beg of next 2 rows—45 (49, 51) sts rem. *Dec row:* (RS) K2, ssk, knit to last 4 sts, k2tog, k2—2 sts dec'd. Dec 1 st each end of needle in this manner every RS row 6 more times—31 (35, 37) sts rem. Work even for ½ (1, 1)" (1.3 [2.5, 2.5] cm), ending with a WS row. BO 9 (10, 10) sts at beg of next 2 rows—13 (15, 17) sts rem. BO all sts.

FINISHING

Weave in loose ends. With yarn threaded on a tapestry needle, sew fronts to back at shoulders. Sew sleeve caps into armholes, matching centers of caps to shoulder seams. Sew sleeve and side seams, allowing edges to curl naturally.

Collar

With smaller needles, WS facing, and beg 3 sts in from center front, pick up and knit 21 sts along left front neck, k22 (24, 26) back neck sts from holder, then pick up and knit 21 sts along right front neck, ending 3 sts before center front—64 (66, 68) sts total. Beg with a knit row, work in St st until piece measures 3½ (4, 4½)" (9 [10, 11.5] cm) from pick-up row. Change to larger needles and work for 1" (2.5 cm) more, ending with a RS row. With WS facing, BO all sts pwise.

Lay garment on a padded surface, such as a terry towel, spritz lightly with water, gently pat into shape, and allow to air-dry. With yarn threaded on a tapestry needle, sew button to left front, opposite buttonhole.

Let the edges roll!

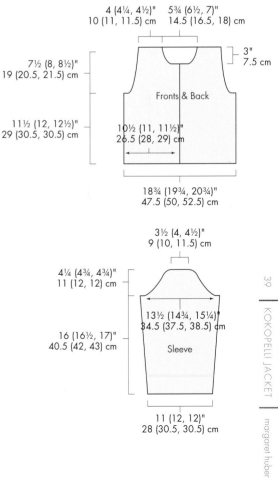

4 (4¼, 4½)"
10 (11, 11.5) cm

5¾ (6½, 7)"
14.5 (16.5, 18) cm

3"
7.5 cm

7½ (8, 8½)"
19 (20.5, 21.5) cm

Fronts & Back

11½ (12, 12½)"
29 (30.5, 30.5) cm

10½ (11, 11½)"
26.5 (28, 29) cm

18¾ (19¾, 20¾)"
47.5 (50, 52.5) cm

3½ (4, 4½)"
9 (10, 11.5) cm

4¼ (4¾, 4¾)"
11 (12, 12) cm

13½ (14¾, 15¼)"
34.5 (37.5, 38.5) cm

16 (16½, 17)"
40.5 (42, 43) cm

Sleeve

11 (12, 12)"
28 (30.5, 30.5) cm

For this colorfully striped pullover, Katie Himmelberg let the yarn do the work for her. The colorwork in the yoke and cuffs is the result of a self-striping yarn that has long color sections. The stripes appeared as Katie knitted—broad stripes where there were fewer stitches, narrow stripes where there were many. Katie worked the body seamlessly in the round from the neck down to the hem. She shaped the yoke in eight sections with paired increases that impart a kaleidoscopic look to the striped pattern. To maintain the simple look, the pullover is worked entirely in stockinette stitch and the edges are allowed to curl naturally.

BODY

With CC and shorter cir needle, CO 80 (80, 80, 80, 88, 88) sts. Place marker (pm) and join for working in the rnd, being careful not to twist sts. Work even in St st (knit all rnds) until piece measures 4" (10 cm) from CO. *Inc rnd:* K4 (4, 4, 4, 5, 5), *M1R (see Glossary), k1 (mark this st with removable marker), M1L (see Glossary), k9 (9, 9, 9, 10, 10); rep from * to last 6 sts, M1R, k1 (mark this st), M1L, k5—96 (96, 96, 96, 104, 104) sts. Knit 4 rnds even. *Inc rnd:* *Knit to marked st, M1R, k1 (marked st), M1L; rep from * 7 more times, knit to end of rnd—16 sts inc'd. Rep the last 5 rnds 9 (10, 12, 14, 16, 18) more times, changing to longer needle as necessary—256 (272, 304, 336, 376, 408) sts. Knit 1 rnd even. Change to MC and knit 2 rnds even—piece measures 11¾ (12½, 13¾, 15¼, 16¾, 18¼)" (30 [31.5, 35, 38.5, 42.5, 46.5] cm) from CO. *Next rnd:* Knit to last 7 (7, 10, 10, 12, 15) sts, slip the next 45 (46, 57, 61, 71, 81) sts onto waste yarn for left sleeve (remove end-of-rnd m), then use the backward-loop method (see Glossary) to CO 8 (10, 10, 8, 6, 6) sts, pm to indicate new beg of rnd, k83 (90, 95, 107, 117, 123), slip the next 45 (46, 57, 61, 71, 81) sts onto waste yarn for right sleeve, use the backward-loop method to CO 8 (10, 10, 8, 6, 6) sts, knit to end—182 (200, 210, 230, 246, 258) sts rem. Work even until piece measures 16 (16, 17, 17, 18, 18)" (40.5 [40.5, 43, 43, 45.5, 45.5] cm) from armhole. Loosely BO all sts.

FINISHED SIZE

About 34¾ (38, 40, 43¾, 46¾, 49¼)" (88.5 [96.5, 101.5, 111, 118.5, 125] cm) bust circumference. Sweater shown measures 38" (96.5 cm).

YARN

DK weight (#3 Light).

Shown here: Schoeller + Stahl Limbo (100% superwash wool; 135 yd [123 m]/50 g): #4587 teal (MC), 5 (6, 6, 7, 8, 9) balls.

Schoeller + Stahl Limbo Color (100% superwash wool; 135 yd [123 m]/50 g): #2539 kolibri (CC), 3 (3, 4, 4, 5, 5) balls.

NEEDLES

Size U.S. 7 (4.5 mm): 12" and 24" (30 and 60 cm) circular (cir). Adjust needle size if necessary to obtain the correct gauge.

NOTIONS

Marker (m); 8 removable markers or safety pins; waste yarn; tapestry needle.

GAUGE

21 stitches and 28 rounds = 4" (10 cm) in stockinette stitch, worked in rounds.

SLEEVES

Place 45 (46, 57, 61, 71, 81) held sleeve sts onto shorter cir needle. Join MC and pick up and knit 1 st in space between held sts and CO sts at underarm, 8 (10, 10, 8, 6, 6) sts along underarm, and 1 st between CO sts and held sts—55 (58, 69, 71, 79, 89) sts total. Work even until piece measures about 16 (16, 17, 17, 17½, 17½)" (40.5 [40.5, 43, 43, 44.5, 44.5] cm) from pick-up rnd. Change to CC and work even for 8" (20.5 cm). Loosely BO all sts.

FINISHING

Weave in loose ends. Block to measurements.

Align decreases
for pattern detail.

Add lots of colors
with a single
variegated yarn.

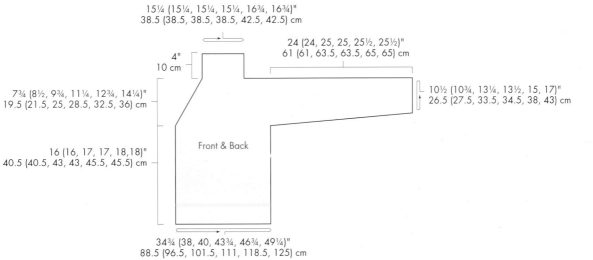

15¼ (15¼, 15¼, 15¼, 16¾, 16¾)"
38.5 (38.5, 38.5, 38.5, 42.5, 42.5) cm

24 (24, 25, 25, 25½, 25½)"
61 (61, 63.5, 63.5, 65, 65) cm

4"
10 cm

7¾ (8½, 9¾, 11¼, 12¾, 14¼)"
19.5 (21.5, 25, 28.5, 32.5, 36) cm

10½ (10¾, 13¼, 13½, 15, 17)"
26.5 (27.5, 33.5, 34.5, 38, 43) cm

Front & Back

16 (16, 17, 17, 18,18)"
40.5 (40.5, 43, 43, 45.5, 45.5) cm

34¾ (38, 40, 43¾, 46¾, 49¼)"
88.5 (96.5, 101.5, 111, 118.5, 125) cm

Kat Coyle worked two identical pieces—one for the front and one for the back—for this breezy little skirt. For each piece, she cast on stitches for the entire length, then worked from one side seam to the other in a series of short-rows to produce the A-line shape (she worked more rows at the hem edge than at the waist edge). The seams at the sides stabilize the pieces and help the skirt hang straight. Kat added columns of eyelets at the lower edge for a feminine touch and finished the hem with a tidy band of I-cord. The waist is finished with a knitted casing for elastic.

NOTE

✦ When working short-rows, pick up and knit wraps together with wrapped stitches on following knit rows.

FINISHED SIZE

About 28 (34, 40, 45½)" (71 [86.5, 101.5, 115.5] cm) waist circumference without elastic and 34 (40, 45½, 51½)" (86.5 [101.5, 115.5, 131] cm) hip circumference, measured 6" (15 cm) below waistband. Skirt shown measures 34" (86.5 cm) at hips.

YARN

DK weight (#3 Light).

Shown here: Rowan Calmer (75% cotton, 25% acrylic microfiber; 175 yd [160 m]/50 g): #461 calm (natural), 6 (7, 8, 9) skeins.

NEEDLES

Body—size U.S. 7 (4.5 mm): 24" (60 cm) circular (cir). Applied I-cord—size U.S. 6 (4 mm): 24" (60 cm) cir. Adjust needle size if necessary to obtain the correct gauge.

NOTIONS

Markers (m); tapestry needle; ¾" (2 cm) non-rolling waistband elastic to measure 1" (2.5 cm) less than actual waist measurement; sharp-point sewing needle; matching sewing thread.

GAUGE

21 stitches and 33 rows = 4" (10 cm) in stockinette stitch on larger needle, after blocking.

Applied I-cord gives a clean finish to the hem.

BACK

With larger needle, CO 115 sts. Do not join. Beg with a WS row, work 3 rows in St st.

*Work 6 rows St st. *Eyelet row:* (RS) K2, [yo, k2tog] 8 times, knit to end. Work 7 (9, 11, 13) rows even in St st. Work short-rows (see Glossary) as foll:

Short-Row 1: (RS) K11, wrap next st, turn.

Short-Rows 2, 4, 6, 8, 10, 12, 14, 16, and 18: (WS) Purl.

Short-Row 3: K22, wrap next st, turn.

Short-Row 5: K33, wrap next st, turn.

Short-Row 7: K44, wrap next st, turn.

Short-Row 9: (Eyelet row) K2, [yo, k2tog] 8 times, k37, wrap next st, turn.

Short-Row 11: K66, wrap next st, turn.

Short-Row 13: K77, wrap next st, turn.

Short-Row 15: K90, wrap next st, turn.

Short-Row 17: K102, wrap next st, turn.

Short-Row 19: K113, wrap next st, turn.

Short-Row 20: Purl.

Work 4 (6, 8, 10) rows even in St st, ending with a WS row. *Next row:* (RS; eyelet row) K2, [yo, k2tog] 8 times, knit to end. Work 9 (11, 13, 15) rows even in St st. Rep from * 3 more times. Knit 1 RS row. With WS facing, BO all sts pwise.

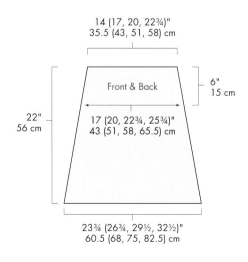

14 (17, 20, 22¾)"
35.5 (43, 51, 58) cm

Front & Back

6"
15 cm

22"
56 cm

17 (20, 22¾, 25¾)"
43 (51, 58, 65.5) cm

23¾ (26¾, 29½, 32½)"
60.5 (68, 75, 82.5) cm

FRONT

CO and work as for back.

FINISHING

Block pieces to measurements. Weave in loose ends. With yarn threaded on a tapestry needle, sew front to back at side seams.

Hem

With smaller cir needle, RS facing, and beg at one side seam, pick up and knit 262 (294, 326, 358) sts evenly spaced around lower edge (pick up about 2 sts for every 3 rows). With RS facing and using the knitted method (see Glossary), CO 3 more sts onto left-hand needle. Work I-cord BO as foll: *K2, k2tog through back loops (tbl), slide the 3 sts from right-hand needle to left-hand needle, pull the working yarn tight across the back; rep from * until 3 sts rem. With yarn threaded on a tapestry needle, sew the 3 rem sts to the CO sts as invisibly as possible.

Waistband

With smaller cir needle, RS facing, and beg at one side seam, pick up and knit 156 (186, 218, 250) sts evenly spaced around waist edge. Place marker (pm) and join for working in rnds. Work even in St st for 1" (2.5 cm). Purl 1 rnd for turning ridge. Work even in St st for 1" (2.5 cm) more for facing. Do not BO. Cut yarn, leaving a tail about 84 (102, 120, 136)" (213.5 [259, 305, 345.5] cm) long. Measure actual waist. Cut waistband elastic 1" (2.5 cm) shorter than actual waist measurement. With sewing needle and thread, sew ends of elastic tog to form a ring. Place elastic ring inside waistband, fold facing to WS along purl ridge, and with long tail threaded on a tapestry needle, sew live sts to WS of pick-up row.

Use short-rows to produce uniform flare.

An expert at knitwear styling, Deborah Newton relied on a simple shape and easy-to-follow stitch patterns in this innovative vest. Deborah worked the front exactly the same way as the back, beginning and ending with an inch of knit-two-purl-two ribbing, and featuring lace and cable patterns in between. She seamed the two pieces together at the sides and partway across the top for the shoulders, leaving a broad opening for the neck, then she finished the armholes with similar ribbing. To give the vest a custom fit, she threaded a knitted drawstring through eyelets in the cable pattern below the bust that can be tied as desired.

STITCH GUIDE

K2, P2 Rib (multiple of 4 sts + 2)
Row 1: (RS) K2, *p2, k2; rep from *.
Row 2: (WS) P2, *k2, p2; rep from *.
Rep Rows 1 and 2 for pattern.

BACK

With smaller needles, CO 122 (134, 150, 166) sts. Work in k2, p2 rib (see Stitch Guide) until piece measures 1" (2.5 cm) from CO, ending with a RS row. *Dec row:* (WS) Work in patt and *at the same time* dec 21 (21, 25, 29) sts as evenly spaced as possible by working k2tog in k2 ribs as presented—101 (113, 125, 137) sts rem. Change to larger needles and work even in St st until piece measures 6½ (7, 7½, 8)" (16.5 [18, 19, 20.5] cm) from CO, ending with a WS row. *Next row:* (RS) K2 (edge sts; work in St st throughout), place marker (pm), beg and ending as indicated for your size, work Row 1 of Lace chart over center 97 (109, 121, 133) sts, pm, k2 (edge sts; work in St st throughout). Work as established through Row 16 of chart, then work Rows 1–13 once more, ending with a RS row. *Inc row:* (WS) P2 (edge sts), k3 (1, 3, 1), *p1, M1P (see Glossary), p2, k5; rep from * to last 8 (6, 8, 6) sts, p1, M1P, p2, k3 (1, 3, 1), p2 (edge sts)—113 (127, 140, 154) sts. Change to smaller needles. Maintaining edge sts and beg and ending as indicated for your size, work center 109 (123, 136, 150) sts according to Rows 1–6 of Eyelet Ribbing chart until this section measures about 6" (15 cm), ending with Row 1 of chart. *Dec row:* (WS) P2 (edge sts), k3 (1, 3, 1), *p1, p2tog, p1, k5; rep from * to last 9 (7, 9, 7) sts, p1, p2tog, p1, k3 (1, 3, 1), p2 (edge sts)—101 (113, 125, 137) sts rem.

FINISHED SIZE

About 31½ (35½, 39, 43)" (80 [90, 99, 109] cm) circumference. Vest shown measures 31½" (80 cm).

YARN

Sportweight (#2 Fine).

Shown here: Louet North America Gems Sport Weight (100% merino; 225 yd [206 m]/100 g) #52 grape, 4 (5, 6, 6) skeins.

NEEDLES

Body—size U.S. 5 (3.75 mm). Edging—size U.S. 4 (3.5 mm). Adjust needle size if necessary to obtain the correct gauge.

NOTIONS

Markers (m); cable needle (cn); tapestry needle.

GAUGE

22 stitches and 31 rows = 4" (10 cm) in stockinette stitch on larger needles.

Use a drawstring to create the fit you want.

Lace

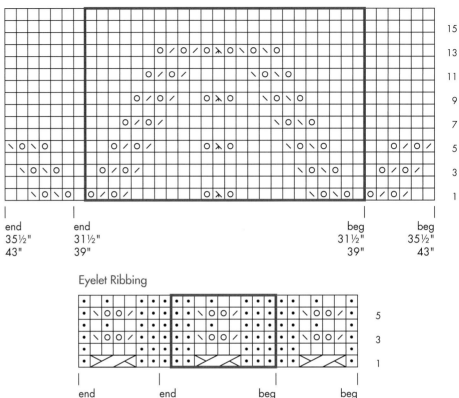

	15
	13
	11
	9
	7
	5
	3
	1

end 35½" 43"   end 31½" 39"   beg 31½" 39"   beg 35½" 43"

Eyelet Ribbing

5
3
1

end 35½" 43"   end 31½" 39"   beg 31½" 39"   beg 35½" 43"

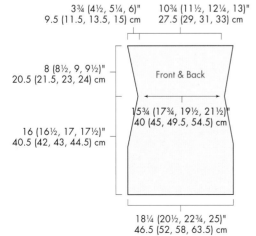

3¾ (4½, 5¼, 6)"
9.5 (11.5, 13.5, 15) cm

10¾ (11½, 12¼, 13)"
27.5 (29, 31, 33) cm

8 (8½, 9, 9½)"
20.5 (21.5, 23, 24) cm

Front & Back

15¾ (17¾, 19½, 21½)"
40 (45, 49.5, 54.5) cm

16 (16½, 17, 17½)"
40.5 (42, 43, 44.5) cm

18¼ (20½, 22¾, 25)"
46.5 (52, 58, 63.5) cm

Legend:

☐	k on RS; p on WS
•	p on RS; k on WS
O	yo
/	k2tog
\	ssk
⅄	sl 1, k2tog, psso
☐	pattern repeat
╳	sl 2 sts onto cn, hold in back, k2, k2 from cn

Change to larger needles. Maintaining edge sts and beg and ending as indicated for your size, work center 97 (109, 121, 133) sts according to Rows 1–16 of Lace chart 2 times (32 rows of chart total), ending with a WS row. Work even in St st until piece measures 23 (24, 25, 26)" (58.5 [61, 63.5, 66 cm] from CO, ending with a RS row. *Next row:* (WS) Purl, inc 21 (21, 25, 29) sts evenly spaced—122 (134, 150, 166) sts. Change to smaller needles and work in k2, p2 rib for 1" (2.5 cm). BO all sts in patt.

FRONT

CO and work as for back.

FINISHING

Weave in loose ends. Block lightly to measurements. With yarn threaded on a tapestry needle, sew front to back at shoulders for 3¾ (4½, 5¼, 6)" (9.5 [11.5, 13.5, 15] cm) each side.

Armhole Edging

Measure down 8 (8½, 9, 9½)" (20.5 [21.5, 23, 24] cm) from shoulder seam on front and back at each side edge for armhole placement. With smaller needle, RS facing, and beg at base of armhole, pick up and knit 98 (102, 110, 114) sts evenly spaced between markers. Work in k2, p2 rib for 1" (2.5 cm). BO all sts in patt. With yarn threaded on a tapestry needle, sew side seams, including base of armhole ribbing.

Tie

With larger needles, CO 300 (325, 350, 375) sts. BO all sts purlwise on next row. Thread tie through desired row of eyelets, beg and end at center front.

Knit two identical pieces
and sew them together.

For this short pullover, Alice Halbeisen designed a twist on the classic V-neck style. She began with a wide band of twisted ribbing (the knit stitches are worked through the back loops) at the hem to draw in the pullover at the waist. Then she extended the ribs in a triangular pattern to the base of the neckline on the front to enhance the slimming look and worked a similar triangular pattern at each sleeve cuff. Alice defined and emphasized the neck and armhole edges with directional decreases that follow the lines of the shaping (called "full-fashioned" shaping). A narrow rolled edge adds a casual finish to the neckband.

STITCH GUIDE

Twisted Rib worked in Rounds (multiple of 2 sts)
All Rnds: *K1 through back loop (tbl), p1; rep from *.

Twisted Rib worked in Rows (multiple of 2 sts + 1)
Row 1: (RS) *K1tbl, p1; rep from * to last st, k1tbl.
Row 2: (WS) *P1tbl, k1; rep from * to last st, p1tbl.
Repeat Rows 1 and 2 for pattern.

NOTES

✢ Once you begin the chart, the rest of the body/sleeve stitches are worked in stockinette stitch.

✢ To lengthen the body, work more rounds of twisted rib before beginning the charted pattern.

FINISHED SIZE
About 30¾ (34, 37¼, 40½, 43½)" (78 [86.5, 94.5, 103, 110.5] cm) bust circumference. To fit bust sizes 30–32 (34–36, 37–39, 40–42, 43–46½)" (76–81.5 [86.5–91.5, 94–99, 101.5–106.5, 109–118] cm). Sweater shown measures 34" (86.5 cm). *Note:* This sweater is designed for a close body-conscious fit.

YARN
DK weight (#3 Light).

Shown here: Filatura di Crosa Zara (100% merino; 137 yd [125 m]/50 g): #1461 burgundy, 7 (8, 9, 9, 10) balls.

NEEDLES
Size U.S. 7 (4.5 mm): 24" (60 cm) circular (cir). Size U.S. 5 (3.75 mm): 24" and 16" (60 and 40 cm) cir. Adjust needle size if necessary to obtain the correct gauge.

NOTIONS
Markers (m); removable marker; stitch holder; tapestry needle.

GAUGE
20 stitches and 27 rounds = 4" (10 cm) in stockinette stitch on smaller needle, worked in rounds; 24 stitches and 27 rounds = 4" (10 cm) in twisted rib pattern on smaller needle, worked in rounds.

Twisted Rib

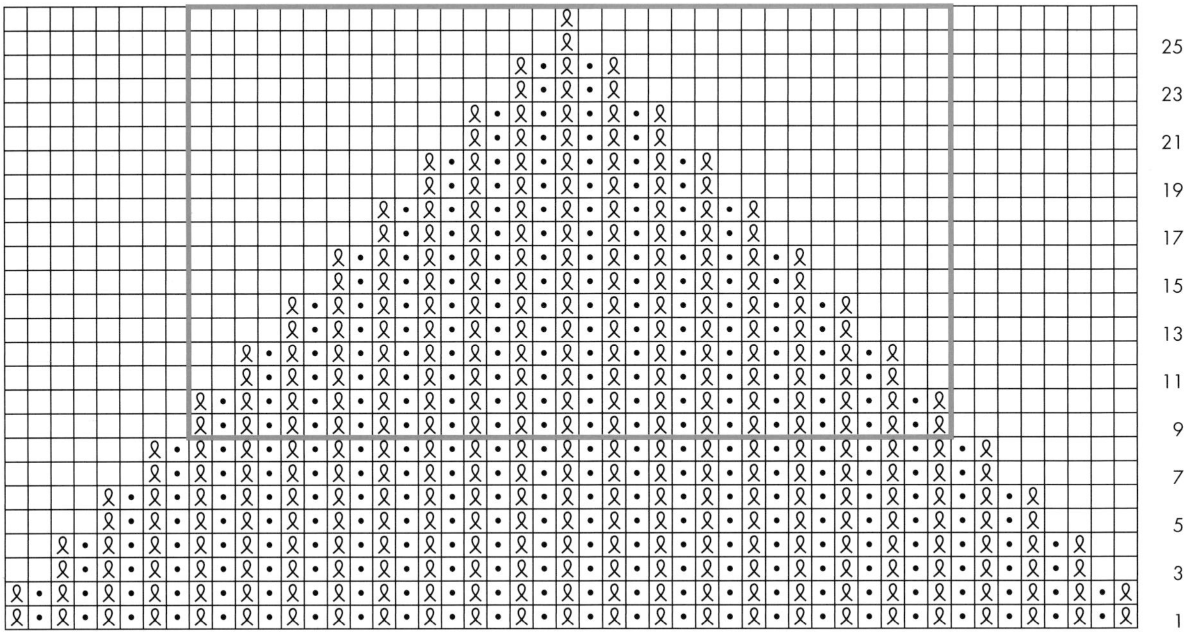

25
23
21
19
17
15
13
11
9
7
5
3
1

	k on RS; p on WS
·	p on RS; k on WS
	k1tbl on RS; p1tbl on WS
—	sleeve chart boundary

3 (3, 3, 3, 3¾)"
7.5 (7.5, 7.5, 7.5, 9.5) cm

Sleeve

4¾ (5¼, 5¾, 5¾, 6¼)"
12 (13.5, 14.5, 14.5, 16) cm

18 (19, 19, 19¼, 19½)"
45.5 (48.5, 48.5, 49, 49.5) cm

10¼ (11, 11¾, 12½, 14½)"
26 (28, 30, 31.5, 37) cm

6¼ (6¼, 6¾, 6¾, 7½)"
16 (16, 17, 17, 19) cm

3¼ (3½, 4, 4, 4½)"
8.5 (9, 10, 10, 11.5) cm

4½ (5, 5, 5¾, 5¾)"
11.5 (12.5, 12.5, 14.5, 14.5) cm

¾"
2 cm

7 (7½, 8, 8, 8½)"
18 (19, 20.5, 20.5, 21.5) cm

Front & Back

7¾ (8¾, 9¼, 9¾, 10¾)"
19.5 (22, 23.5, 25, 27.5) cm

12 (12½, 12½, 13, 13½)"
30.5 (31.5, 31.5, 33, 34.5) cm

30¾ (34, 37¼, 40½, 43½)"
78 (86.5, 94.5, 103, 110.5) cm

25¾ (28¼, 31, 33¾, 36¼)"
65.5 (72, 78.5, 85.5, 92) cm

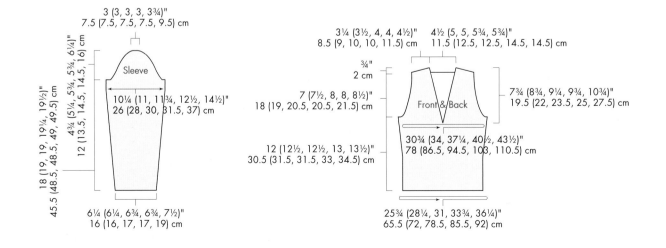

LOWER BODY

With larger needle, CO 154 (170, 186, 202, 218) sts. Place marker (pm) and join for working in rnds, being careful not to twist sts. *Next rnd:* Work twisted rib (see Stitch Guide) across 77 (85, 93, 101, 109) sts for front, pm (it's helpful to use a marker of a different color here), beg with a purl st, cont in patt to end—77 (85, 93, 101, 109) sts each for front and back. Work even as established until piece measures 2" (5 cm) from CO. Change to smaller 24" (60 cm) cir needle. Cont as established until piece measures 7" (18 cm) from CO. *Set-up rnd:* K14 (18, 22, 26, 30), pm, work next 49 sts according to Row 1 of Twisted Rib chart, pm, knit to end of rnd. Cont as established through Row 26 of chart. Knit 2 rnds—piece measures about 11¼" (28.5 cm) from CO.

Shape V-Neck

K38 (42, 46, 50, 54) for left front, place removable marker through next st and remove it from needle, turn work. Working back and forth in rows (center front is beg of row), purl 1 row. *Next row:* (RS) K1, ssk (see Glossary), knit to last 3 sts, k2tog, k1—2 neck sts dec'd. Dec 1 st at each neck edge in this manner every 4th row 10 (11, 11, 13, 13) more times and *at the same time* when piece measures 12 (12½, 12½, 13, 13½)" (30.5 [31.5, 31.5, 33, 34.5] cm) from CO, on a RS row, knit to right underarm, join a second ball of yarn and knit to left underarm, place the last 77 (85, 93, 101, 109) sts worked on holder for back, knit to end of row.

FRONT

Shape Armholes

Working each side separately and cont to work neck shaping as established, at each armhole edge, BO 4 (5, 5, 6, 6) sts once, then BO 2 (2, 3, 3, 4) sts once, then dec 1 st every RS row 5 (5, 6, 7, 8) times—16 (18, 20, 20, 22) sts rem each side when all armhole and neck shaping is complete. Work even until armholes measure 7 (7½, 8, 8, 8½)" (18 [19, 20.5, 20.5, 21.5] cm).

Shape Shoulders

At each armhole edge, BO 5 (6, 6, 6, 7) sts 2 times, then BO rem 6 (6, 8, 8, 8) sts.

BACK

Return 77 (85, 93, 101, 109) back sts to smaller cir needle. Rejoin yarn with RS facing.

Shape Armholes

BO 4 (5, 5, 6, 6) sts at beg of next 2 rows, then BO 2 (2, 3, 3, 4) sts at beg of foll 2 rows—65 (71, 77, 83, 89) sts rem. Dec 1 st each end of needle every RS row 5 (5, 6, 7, 8) times—55 (61, 65, 69, 73) sts rem. Work even until armholes measure 7 (7½, 8, 8, 8½)" (18 [19, 20.5, 20.5, 21.5] cm), ending with a RS row.

A decorative twisted rib adds visual interest and a slimming fit.

Sometimes a simple design is simply fantastic!

Shape Neck and Shoulders

(WS) P18 (20, 22, 22, 24), join a second ball of yarn and p19 (21, 21, 25, 25), place the last 19 (21, 21, 25, 25) sts worked on holder, purl to end—18 (20, 22, 22, 24) sts rem each side. Working each side separately, dec 1 st at each neck edge every RS row 2 times and *at the same time* at each armhole edge BO 5 (6, 6, 6, 7) sts 2 times, then BO rem 6 (6, 8, 8, 8) sts.

SLEEVES

With smaller cir needle, CO 37 (37, 41, 41, 45) sts. Do not join. Work back and forth in twisted rib until piece measures 1½" (3.8 cm), ending with a WS row. *Next row:* (RS) K2 (2, 4, 4, 6), work next 33 sts according to sleeve portion of Twisted Rib chart (beg on chart Row 9), k2 (2, 4, 4, 6). Work as established through Row 26 of chart—18 chart rows worked. Change to St st. Work 2 rows even. *Inc row:* (RS) K1, M1 (see Glossary), knit to last st, M1, k1—2 sts inc'd. Inc 1 st each end of needle in this manner every 4th row 0 (2, 2, 1, 2) more time(s), then every 6th row 6 (6, 6, 9, 11) times—51 (55, 59, 63, 73) sts. Work even until piece measures 18 (19, 19, 19¼, 19½)" (45.5 [48.5, 48.5, 49, 49.5] cm) from CO or desired length to armhole, ending with a WS row.

Shape Cap

BO 4 (5, 5, 6, 6) sts at beg of next 2 rows, then BO 2 (2, 3, 3, 4) sts at beg of foll 2 rows—39 (41, 43, 45, 53) sts rem. Dec 1 st each end of needle every 4th row 1 (2, 0, 0, 2) time(s), then every RS row 7 (7, 8, 9, 9) times—23 (23, 27, 27, 31) sts rem. Work even until cap measures 4½ (5, 5½, 5½, 6)" (11.5 [12.5, 14, 14, 15] cm), ending with a WS row. BO 4 (4, 6, 6, 6) sts at beg of next 2 rows—15 (15, 15, 15, 19) sts rem. BO all sts.

FINISHING

Block pieces to measurements. Weave in loose ends.

Seams

With yarn threaded on a tapestry needle, sew front to back at shoulders. Sew sleeve caps into armholes, matching centers of caps to shoulder seams. Sew sleeve seams.

Neckband

With shorter cir needle, RS facing, and beg at left shoulder seam, pick up and purl (see Glossary) 39 (44, 47, 49, 54) sts (about 3 sts for every 4 rows) along left front neck, purl marked center st, pick up and purl 39 (44, 47, 49, 54) sts along right front neck to shoulder, 3 sts to back neck holder, p19 (21, 21, 25, 25) back neck sts from holder, pick up and purl 3 sts to shoulder—104 (116, 122, 130, 140) sts total. Pm and join for working in rnds. *Dec rnd:* Knit to 2 sts before marked center st, k2tog, k1 (marked center st), ssk, knit to end—2 sts dec'd. Rep dec rnd every rnd 3 more times. BO all sts kwise.

The overall shape may be loose and boxy, but Vicki Square proves once again that a kimono makes a flattering silhouette when draped on a female body. In this classic version, she worked the back as a rectangle and the fronts as modified rectangles to accommodate the deep V-neck shaping. To reduce the number of seams, Vicki used a three-needle bind-off at the shoulders and she worked the sleeves downward from stitches picked up at the armholes. A subtle knit-three-purl-one rib prevents curling at the hem and cuffs while maintaining the clean look of the stockinette-stitch body. The neckband, worked separately in a firm knit-one-purl-one rib, is sewn to the shaped neckline and hangs free below the knitted tab closure.

NOTE
✦ Blocking will relax the yarn and give a beautiful drape, but it may cause the pieces to lengthen by about 1" (2.5 cm).

FINISHED SIZE
About 46½ (54)" (118 [137] cm) bust circumference, fastened. Kimono shown measures 46½" (118 cm).

YARN
Worsted weight (#4 Medium).
Shown here: Berroco Softwist (59% rayon, 41% wool; 100 yd [91 m]/50 g): #9479 turquoise, 16 (19) skeins.

NEEDLES
Body and sleeves—size U.S. 8 (5 mm): 24" (60 cm) circular (cir), plus one extra for three-needle bind-off. Neckband and closure—size U.S. 7 (4.5 mm): straight. Adjust needle size if necessary to obtain the correct gauge.

NOTIONS
Stitch holders; markers (m); removable markers or safety pins; tapestry needle.

GAUGE
18 stitches and 25 rows = 4" (10 cm) in stockinette stitch on larger needle, after blocking.

BACK
With larger cir needle and using the long-tail method (see Glossary), CO 105 (121) sts. Do not join. Work back and forth in rows as foll:
Row 1: (WS) *K1, p3; rep from * to last st, k1.
Row 2: (RS) *P1, k3; rep from * to last st, p1.
Rep these 2 rows once more, then work Row 1 again—5 rows total. Change to St st and work even until piece measures 26 (28½)" (66 [72.5] cm) from CO, ending with a WS row. Place sts on holder.

Right Front
With larger cir needle and using the long-tail method, CO 64 (72) sts. Do not join. Work back and forth in rows as foll:
Row 1: (WS) [K1, p3] 14 (16) times, place marker (pm), [k1, p1] 4 times.

Use a three-needle bind-off instead of sewing shoulder seams.

Row 2: (RS) Sl 1 pwise with yarn in back (wyb), p1, [k1, p1] 3 times, slip marker (sl m), *k3, p1; rep from *.

Rep these 2 rows once more, then work Row 1 again—5 rows total. *Next row:* (RS) Sl 1 pwise wyb, p1, [k1, p1] 3 times, sl m, knit to end. *Next row:* (WS) Purl to m, sl m, [k1, p1] 4 times. Rep the last 2 rows until piece measures 8 (9)" (20.5 [23] cm) from CO, ending with a WS row.

Shape Neck

(RS) K1, ssk (see Glossary), work in rib to m, knit to end of row—1 st dec'd. Keeping in patt, dec 1 st at neck edge in this manner every 4th row 27 (30) more times, removing m when all rib sts have been dec'd—36 (41) sts rem. Cont even in St st until piece measures 26 (28½)" (66 [72.5] cm) from CO, ending with a WS row. Place sts on holder.

LEFT FRONT

With larger cir needle and using the long-tail method, CO 64 (72) sts. Do not join. Work back and forth in rows as foll:

Row 1: (WS) Sl 1 pwise with yarn in front (wyf), [k1, p1] 3 times, k1, pm, [p3, k1] 14 (16) times.
Row 2: (RS) [P1, k3] 14 (16) times, sl m, [p1, k1] 4 times.

Rep these 2 rows once more, then work Row 1 again—5 rows total. *Next row:* (RS) Knit to m, sl m, [p1, k1] 4 times. *Next row:* (WS) Sl 1 pwise wyf, [k1, p1] 3 times, k1, sl m, purl to end. Rep the last 2 rows until piece measures 8 (9)" (20.5 [23] cm) from CO, ending with a WS row.

Shape Neck

(RS) Work as established to last 3 sts, k2tog, k1—1 st dec'd. Keeping in patt, dec 1 st at neck edge in this manner every 4th row 27 (30) more times, removing m when all rib sts have been dec'd—36 (41) sts rem. Cont even in St st until piece measures 26 (28½)" (66 [72.5] cm) from CO, ending with a WS row. Place sts on holder.

JOIN FRONTS TO BACK AT SHOULDERS

Place 105 (121) back sts onto one needle and 36 (41) right front sts onto another needle. With RS tog and using the three-needle method (see Glossary), BO 36 (41) right front sts to back. BO next 33 (39) back sts individually for back neck. Place 36 (41) left front sts onto spare needle and, with RS tog, BO left front to rem back sts. Cut yarn and pull tail through last st to secure.

SLEEVES

Measure 12 (12¾)" (30.5 [32.5] cm) down from shoulder seam on armhole edge of front and back and mark for sleeve placement. With larger needle, RS facing, and beg at base of armhole, pick up and knit 114 (120) sts evenly spaced between markers. Knit 1 WS row. *Dec row:* (RS) K1, k2tog, knit to last 3 sts, ssk, k1—2 sts dec'd. Dec 1 st each end of needle in this manner every 4th row 18 (19) more times, ending with a RS row—76 (80) sts rem. *Next row:* (WS) [P17 (18), p2tog] 3 times, purl to end—73 (77) sts rem.

Cuff

Row 1: (RS) *P1, k3; rep from * to last st, p1.

Row 2: (WS) *K1, p3; rep from * to last st, k1.

Rep these 2 rows 3 more times—8 rows total. With RS facing, BO all sts in patt.

FINISHING

Weave in loose ends. Lay the pieces flat and place a wet towel over them to block.

Neckband

With smaller needles, CO 20 sts. *Next row:* Sl 1 pwise wyb, p1, *k1, p1; rep from *. Rep this row until piece measures 8 (9)" (20.5 [23] cm) from CO, ending with a WS row. Place removable marker at left edge (edge that will be sewn to body). Cont as foll:

Row 1: (RS) Sl 1 pwise wyb, p1, *k1, p1; rep from *.

Row 2: (WS) *K1, p1; rep from *.

Rep these 2 rows until piece measures 51¾ (57¼)" (131.5 [145.5] cm) from CO, slightly stretched. Place another removable marker at left edge. Rep Row 1 until piece measures 8 (9)" (20.5 [23] cm) from last marker. BO all sts in patt.

Closure Tab

With smaller needles, CO 20 sts. Knit 1 row. Firmly BO all sts (to encourage piece to curve naturally).

Drapy yarn and a loose fit team up for an elegant silhouette.

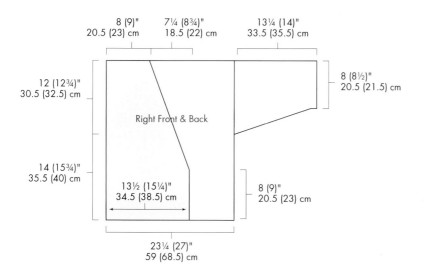

Seams

With yarn threaded on a tapestry needle and using a ½-st seam allowance, use the mattress st (see Glossary) to sew side and sleeve seams. Pin non-slipped st edge of neckband to neck edge, matching the first neckband marker to the first dec on right front, and the second neckband marker to the first dec on left front. With yarn threaded on a tapestry needle and using a ½-st seam allowance on body and catching the edge purl st of neckband, sew neckband in place between markers. Sew one end of closure tab to right front about 9½ (10½)" (24 [26.5] cm) from lower edge and just inside the center front rib; sew the other end 10½ (11½)" (26.5 [29] cm) from lower edge and about 3" (7.5 cm) toward side seam from first end.

With WS facing, lightly steam-block neckband seam (not ribbed portion of neckband).

This sweater vest complements every figure by stretching in just the right places. Ruthie Nussbaum worked the body in stockinette stitch with wide bands of knit-one-purl-one ribbing along each side to ensure a perfect fit for every body type. She worked the body in the round from the hem to the base of the V-neck, then worked the fronts and back separately to the shoulders. To maintain the continuity of the rib pattern at the underarms, Ruthie shaped the armholes with a series of short-rows. She finished the neckline with knit-two-purl-two ribbing that crosses at the base of the V. She included a ribbed belt for added style.

BODY

With larger cir needle, CO 18 (20, 22, 22, 26) sts, place marker (pm), CO 68 (72, 84, 92, 100) more sts, pm, CO 18 (20, 22, 22, 26) more sts, pm, CO 68 (72, 84, 92, 100) more sts—172 (184, 212, 228, 252) sts total. Pm and join for working in rnds, being careful not to twist sts. *Next rnd:* *K1, p1; rep from * to first m, slip marker (sl m), **k2, p2; rep from ** to next marker, sl m; rep from *. Rep this rnd 7 more times—8 rnds total. *Next rnd:* *K1, p1; rep from * to first m, sl m, knit to next m, sl m; rep from *. Cont in patt as established (knit the knits and purl the purls) until piece measures 13½ (14, 14½, 14½, 15)" (34.5 [35.5, 37, 37, 38] cm) from CO.

Shape V-Neck

Note: The armhole shaping is introduced at the same time as the neck is shaped; read all the way through the foll sections before proceeding. *K1, p1; rep from * to first m, sl m, k34 (36, 42, 46, 50) to the center front. Working back and forth in rows (center front is beg of row) and maintaining the patt as established, work 1 WS row. *Dec row:* (RS) K1, k2tog, work as established to last 3 sts, ssk (see Glossary), k1—2 sts dec'd. Work 3 rows even in patt. Rep the last 4 rows 19 (19, 20, 21, 22) more times. *At the same time* when piece measures 16½ (17, 17½, 17½, 18)" (42 [43, 44.5, 44.5, 45.5] cm) from CO, shape armholes as foll.

Back

With RS facing, work to first marker, work next 4 (4, 6, 6, 6) sts in rib as established. Place the sts just worked onto a holder or waste yarn to work later for right front, work next 10 (12, 10, 10, 14) sts as established and place these 10 (12, 10, 10, 14) sts on another holder or

FINISHED SIZE

29¼ (31¼, 36, 39, 42¾)" (74.5 [79.5, 91.5, 99, 108.5] cm) bust circumference. To fit bust sizes 32 (34, 39, 42, 46)" (81.5 [86.5, 99, 106.5, 117] cm). *Note:* This vest has a snug body-conscious fit. Vest shown measures 31¼" (79.5 cm).

YARN

DK weight (#3 Light).

Shown here: GGH Maxima (100% merino wool; 120 yd [110 m]/50 g): #10 dijon, 6 (7, 8, 9, 10) balls.

NEEDLES

Body—U.S. size 6 (4 mm): 24" (60 cm) circular (cir). Edging—size U.S. 5 (3.75 mm): 16" (40 cm) cir. Adjust needle size if necessary to obtain the correct gauge.

NOTIONS

Markers (m); stitch holders; tapestry needle.

GAUGE

22 stitches and 31 rows = 4" (10 cm) in stockinette stitch on larger needle.

waste yarn for underarm, work next 4 (4, 6, 6, 6) sts in rib as established, k68 (72, 84, 92, 100) back sts, work 4 (4, 6, 6, 6) sts in rib as established, place next 10 (12, 10, 10, 14) sts on holder for underarm, place rem sts on holder for left front—76 (80, 96, 104, 112) back sts total. Work short-rows (see Glossary) as foll:

Short-Row 1: (WS) Work 4 (4, 6, 6, 6) sts in rib, p68 (72, 84, 92, 100), work 2 (2, 4, 4, 4) sts in rib, wrap next st, turn.

Short-Row 2: (RS) Work 2 (2, 4, 4, 4) sts in rib, k68 (72, 84, 92, 100), work 2 (2, 4, 4, 4) sts in rib, wrap next st, turn.

Short-Row 3: (WS) Work 2 (2, 4, 4, 4) sts in rib, p68 (72, 84, 92, 100), work 0 (0, 2, 2, 2) sts in rib, wrap next st, turn.

Short-Row 4: (RS) Work 0 (0, 2, 2, 2) sts in rib, k68 (72, 84, 92, 100), work 0 (0, 2, 2, 2) sts in rib, wrap next st, turn.

This completes the short-row shaping for sizes 29¼ (31¼)".

Sizes (36, 39, 42¾)" only

Short-Row 5: (WS) Work (2, 2, 2) sts in rib, p(84, 92, 100), wrap next st, turn.

Short-Row 6: (RS) K(84, 92, 100), wrap next st, turn.

All Sizes

Place rib sts at each end of needle on holder with other underarm rib sts—68 (72, 84, 92, 100) sts rem for back. Dec 1 st each end of needle every RS row 4 (5, 8, 11, 13) times—60 (62, 68, 70, 74) sts rem. Work even in St st until armholes measure 8 (8½, 9, 9½, 10)" (20.5 [21.5, 23, 24, 25.5] cm), ending with a WS row.

Shape Shoulders

Mark center 40 (40, 42, 44, 46) sts for neck. BO 3 (3, 4, 4, 5) sts, knit to marked center sts, place next 40 (40, 42, 44, 46) sts on holder for neck, place foll 10 (11, 13, 13, 14) sts on holder for left shoulder—7 (8, 9, 9, 9) sts rem for right shoulder. Purl 1 WS row. BO 4 (4, 4, 4, 5) sts at beg of next RS row—3 (4, 5, 5, 4) sts rem. Purl 1 WS row. BO all sts. With RS facing, join yarn to left back shoulder and knit to end of row. BO 3 (3, 4, 4, 5) sts on next row, then BO 4 (4, 4, 4, 5) sts on foll WS row—3 (4, 5, 5, 4) sts rem. Knit 1 RS row. With WS facing, BO all sts.

LEFT FRONT

With RS facing, place held left front sts on needle. Cont to dec at neck as established, work 1 RS row. Work short-rows at armhole edge as foll, beg with a WS row:

Short-Row 1: (WS) Purl to m, work 2 (2, 4, 4, 4) sts in rib, wrap next st, turn.

Next row: (RS) Work 2 (2, 4, 4, 4) sts in rib, work to end.

This completes the short-row shaping for sizes 29¼ (31¼").

Sizes (36, 39, 42¾)" only

Short-Row 2: (WS) Purl to m, work (2, 2, 2) sts in rib, wrap next st, turn.

Next row: (RS) Work (2, 2, 2) sts in rib, work to end.

All Sizes

Place rib sts on holder with other underarm sts.

Dec 1 st at beg of every RS row 4 (5, 8, 11, 13) times—10 (11, 13, 13, 14) sts rem after all armhole and neck shaping is complete. Work even until armhole measures 8 (8½, 9, 9½, 10)" (20.5 [21.5, 23, 24, 25.5] cm), ending with a WS row.

Shape Shoulder

BO 3 (3, 4, 4, 5) sts at beg of next (RS) row, then BO 4 (4, 4, 4, 5) sts at beg of foll RS row—3 (4, 5, 5, 4) sts rem. BO all sts on next RS row.

Ribs along the sides ensure a flattering fit for every body.

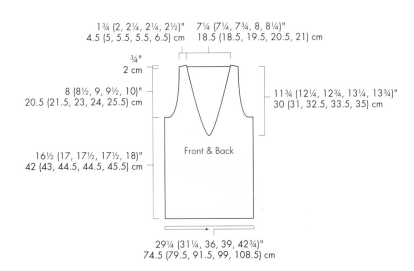

1¾ (2, 2¼, 2¼, 2½)"
4.5 (5, 5.5, 5.5, 6.5) cm

7¼ (7¼, 7¾, 8, 8¼)"
18.5 (18.5, 19.5, 20.5, 21) cm

¾"
2 cm

8 (8½, 9, 9½, 10)"
20.5 (21.5, 23, 24, 25.5) cm

11¾ (12¼, 12¾, 13¼, 13¾)"
30 (31, 32.5, 33.5, 35) cm

Front & Back

16½ (17, 17½, 17½, 18)"
42 (43, 44.5, 44.5, 45.5) cm

29¼ (31¼, 36, 39, 42¾)"
74.5 (79.5, 91.5, 99, 108.5) cm

RIGHT FRONT

With WS facing, place held right front sts on needle. Work 1 WS row. Cont to dec at neck as established, work short-rows at armhole edge as foll, beg with a RS row:

Short-Row 1: (RS) Work to m, work 2 (2, 4, 4, 4) sts in rib, wrap next st, turn.

Next row: (WS) Work 2 (2, 4, 4, 4) sts in rib, purl to end.

This completes the short-row shaping for sizes 29¼ (31¼)".

Sizes (36, 39, 42¾)" only

Short-Row 2: (RS) Work to m, work (2, 2, 2) sts in rib, wrap next st, turn.

Next row: (WS) Work (2, 2, 2) sts in rib, purl to end.

All Sizes

Place rib sts on holder with other underarm sts. Dec 1 st at end of every RS row 4 (5, 8, 11, 13) times—10 (11, 13, 13, 14) sts rem after all armhole and neck shaping is complete. Work even until armhole measures 8 (8½, 9, 9½, 10)" (20.5 [21.5, 23, 24, 25.5] cm), ending with a RS row.

Shape Shoulder

BO 3 (3, 4, 4, 5) sts at beg of next (WS) row, then BO 4 (4, 4, 4, 5) sts at beg of foll WS row—3 (4, 5, 5, 4) sts rem. BO all sts on next WS row.

FINISHING

Block pieces lightly. Weave in loose ends. With yarn threaded on a tapestry needle, sew fronts to back at shoulders.

Neckband

With smaller cir needle, RS facing, and beg at base of V, pick up and knit 68 (72, 75, 80, 83) sts evenly spaced along right front neck edge to shoulder, 4 sts along back neck to holder, k40 (40, 42, 44, 46) back neck sts from holder, pick up and knit 4 sts along back neck to shoulder, and 68 (72, 75, 80, 83) sts along left front neck edge—184 (192, 200, 212, 220) sts total. Working back and forth in rows, work in k2, p2 rib for 8 rows. BO all sts in patt. With yarn threaded on a tapestry needle, sew edges of band in place at base of V.

Armhole Ribbing

Place 18 (20, 22, 22, 26) underarm sts on smaller cir needle, pm, and with RS facing, join yarn and pick up and knit 88 (96, 104, 112, 120) sts evenly spaced around armhole—106 (116, 126, 134, 146) sts total. Pm and join for working in rnds. *Set-up rnd:* Working wraps tog with wrapped sts, work in k1, p1 rib to first marker, work in k2, p2 rib to end of rnd. Cont as established for 5 more rnds. BO all sts in patt.

Belt

With larger needle, CO 12 sts. Do not join for working in rnds. *Set-up row:* Sl 1, *p1, k1; rep from * to last st, p1. Slipping the first st of every row, cont in rib as established until piece measures 42 (44, 48, 52, 56)" (106.5 [112, 122, 132, 142] cm) from CO. BO all sts in patt.

A ribbed belt is completely reversible.

Therese Chynoweth included a lot of details in this swingy cardigan, but none is difficult, and the overall effect is simply beautiful. She worked the lower body in a single piece to the armholes, then worked the back and fronts separately to the shoulders. She also worked the sleeves in the round to the armholes, but she shaped the caps while working back and forth in rows. To produce the swingy drape, Therese knitted the wide ribs in the lower body on larger needles and tapered them at the base of the drawstring closure. Decorative buttons and buttonbands keep the bodice fastened while the "skirt" hangs freely. The neck and cuffs are edged with a few rows of garter stitch.

STITCH GUIDE

sssk (worked over 3 sts)
Sl 3 sts individually kwise, insert left needle tip in the front of these 3 sts and knit them tog through their back loops—1 st rem.

BODY

With larger 32" (80 cm) cir needle, CO 253 (273, 313, 353, 393) sts. Do not join. *Set-up row:* (RS) K4, *p5, k5; rep from * to last 9 sts, p5, k4. Cont in rib patt as established (knit the knits and purl the purls) until piece measures 12 (12, 12¼, 12¼, 12½)" (30.5 [30.5, 31, 31, 31.5] cm) from CO, ending with a WS row. Change to smaller 32" (80 cm) cir needle. *Dec row:* (RS) *K3, sssk (see Stitch Guide), k1, k3tog; rep from * to last 3 sts, k3—153 (165, 189, 213, 237) sts rem. Purl 1 WS row, placing markers (pm) after the first 35 (38, 44, 50, 56) sts and again after the next 83 (89, 101, 113, 125) sts—35 (38, 44, 50, 56) sts for each front; 83 (89, 101, 113, 125) sts for back. *Eyelet row:* (RS) K2, yo, k2tog, k3, *yo, k2tog, k4; rep from * to last 8 sts, yo, k2tog, k3, yo, k2tog, k1. Work even in St st (knit RS rows; purl WS rows) until piece measures 17 (17¼, 17½, 17¾, 18)" (43 [44, 44.5, 45, 45.5] cm) from CO, ending with a WS row.

FINISHED SIZE
About 33 (35½, 40½, 45, 50)" (84 [90, 103, 114.5, 127] cm) bust circumference, buttoned. Cardigan shown measures 35½" (90 cm).

YARN
DK weight (#3 Light).
Shown here: Dale of Norway Lerke (52% merino, 48% cotton; 126 yd [115 m]/50 g): #2641 khaki, 8 (9, 11, 12, 13) balls.

NEEDLES
Upper body and sleeves—size U.S. 6 (4 mm): 16" (40 cm) and 32" (80 cm) circular (cir) and set of 4 or 5 double-pointed (dpn). Ribbing—size U.S. 7 (4.5 mm): 32" (80 cm) cir. Adjust needle size if necessary to obtain the correct gauge.

NOTIONS
Markers (m); tapestry needle; size G/6 (4 mm) crochet hook; four (four, four, four, five) ⅞" (2.2 cm) buttons.

GAUGE
20 stitches and 27 rounds or rows = 4" (10 cm) in stockinette stitch on smaller needle.

Shape Armholes

K32 (35, 41, 47, 53), join a second ball of yarn and BO 6 sts for right armhole, knit to 3 sts before m, join another ball of yarn and BO 6 sts for left armhole, knit to end—32 (35, 41, 47, 53) sts for each front; 77 (83, 95, 107, 119) sts for back. Working each piece separately, at each armhole edge BO 2 sts 2 (2, 2, 3, 3) times, then BO 1 st 1 (3, 6, 6, 9) time(s)—27 (28, 31, 35, 38) sts rem for each front; 67 (69, 75, 83, 89) sts rem for back. Work even until armholes measure 3¾ (3¾, 4, 4, 4¼)" (9.5 [9.5, 10, 10, 11] cm).

Shape Neck

Note: The back neck shaping is introduced while the front neck shaping is being worked; read all the way through the next sections before proceeding.

Front Neck

At each neck edge, BO 2 sts once—25 (26, 29, 33, 36) sts rem for each front. Dec 1 st at each neck edge every RS row 6 (6, 6, 7, 7) times, then every 4th row 2 (3, 3, 3, 3) times—17 (17, 20, 23, 26) sts rem for each front. *At the same time* when armholes measure 6¾ (7, 7¼, 7½, 7¾)" (17 [18, 18.5, 19, 19.5] cm), shape back neck.

Back Neck

(RS) K22 (22, 25, 28, 31), join a second ball of yarn and BO 23 (25, 25, 27, 27) sts for back neck, knit to end—22 (22, 25, 28, 31) sts rem for each side of back. Working each side separately, at each neck edge BO 3 sts once, then BO 2 sts once—17 (17, 20, 23, 26) sts rem each side. Work even until armholes measure 7½ (7¾, 8, 8¼, 8½)" (19 [19.5, 20.5, 21, 21.5] cm), ending with a WS row. BO all sts.

To eliminate side and sleeve seams, work the lower body and sleeves in the round.

SLEEVES

With smaller dpn, CO 39 (39, 43, 47, 47) sts. Pm and join for working in rnds, being careful not to twist sts. Purl 1 rnd. Knit 1 rnd. Purl 1 rnd. Cont in St st and *at the same time* inc 1 st each side of marker every 4th rnd 0 (2, 4, 5, 11) times, then every 6th rnd 10 (16, 15, 15, 11) times, then every 8th rnd 5 (0, 0, 0, 0) times—69 (75, 81, 87, 91) sts. Work even until piece measures 16 (16½, 17, 17½, 17½)" (40.5 [42, 43, 44.5, 44.5] cm) from CO, ending last rnd 3 sts before m.

Shape Cap

BO 6 sts, knit to end—63 (69, 75, 81, 85) sts rem. Cont working back and forth in rows, BO 3 sts at beg of next 2 rows, then BO 2 sts at beg of foll 6 rows, then BO 1 st at beg of foll 20 (22, 22, 24, 24) rows—25 (29, 35, 39, 43) sts rem. BO 2 sts at beg of next 2 (4, 4, 4, 4) rows, then BO 3 sts at beg of foll 2 rows—15 (15, 21, 25, 29) sts rem. BO all sts.

Use larger needles to offset the draw-in of ribbing.

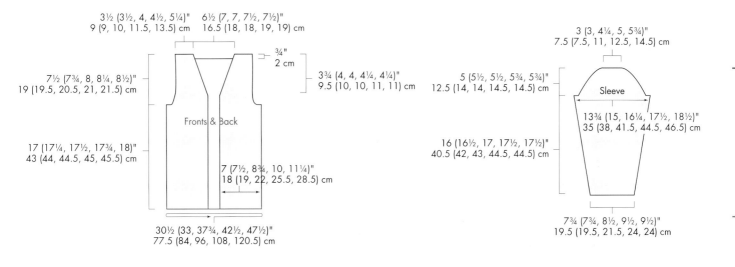

3½ (3½, 4, 4½, 5¼)"
9 (9, 10, 11.5, 13.5) cm

6½ (7, 7, 7½, 7½)"
16.5 (18, 18, 19, 19) cm

¾"
2 cm

7½ (7¾, 8, 8¼, 8½)"
19 (19.5, 20.5, 21, 21.5) cm

3¾ (4, 4, 4¼, 4¼)"
9.5 (10, 10, 11, 11) cm

Fronts & Back

17 (17¼, 17½, 17¾, 18)"
43 (44, 44.5, 45, 45.5) cm

7 (7½, 8¾, 10, 11¼)"
18 (19, 22, 25.5, 28.5) cm

30½ (33, 37¾, 42½, 47½)"
77.5 (84, 96, 108, 120.5) cm

3 (3, 4¼, 5, 5¾)"
7.5 (7.5, 11, 12.5, 14.5) cm

5 (5½, 5½, 5¾, 5¾)"
12.5 (14, 14, 14.5, 14.5) cm

Sleeve

13¾ (15, 16¼, 17½, 18½)"
35 (38, 41.5, 44.5, 46.5) cm

16 (16½, 17, 17½, 17½)"
40.5 (42, 43, 44.5, 44.5) cm

7¾ (7¾, 8½, 9½, 9½)"
19.5 (19.5, 21.5, 24, 24) cm

FINISHING

Block pieces to measurements. With yarn threaded on a tapestry needle, sew fronts to back at shoulders.

Left Front Edging

With smaller 32" (80 cm) cir needle and RS facing, pick up and knit 41 (41, 41, 41, 46) sts to top of rib, pm, pick up and knit 59 (59, 60, 60, 61) sts to lower edge—100 (100, 101, 101, 107) sts total. Purl 1 WS row. *Eyelet row:* (RS) *K2, k2tog, yo, k1; rep from * to 1 st before m, k1, BO pwise to end of row—41 (41, 41, 41, 46) sts rem. With WS facing, rejoin yarn to rem sts and work even in St st until placket measures about 1" (2.5 cm) from pick-up row, ending with a RS row. Knit 2 rows. BO all sts kwise. Mark placement for buttons so that the top button is ⅝" (1.5 cm) below the top of the placket, the bottom button is ⅝" (1.5 cm) above the bottom of the placket, and the others are evenly spaced in between.

Right Front Edging

With smaller 32" (80 cm) cir needle and RS facing, pick up and knit 59 (59, 60, 60, 61) sts along right front edge to top of rib, pm, pick up and knit 41 (41, 41, 41, 46) sts to top of front—100 (100, 101, 101, 107) sts total. Purl 1 WS row. *Eyelet row:* (RS) BO pwise to m, *k1, yo, k2tog, k2; rep from to end—41 (41, 41, 41, 46) sts rem. Work even in St st until placket measures about 1" (2.5 cm) from pick-up row, ending with a RS row. Knit 1 WS row. *Buttonhole row:* (RS) Knit and *at the same time* work a 3-st one-row buttonhole (see Glossary) opposite each button marker on left front placket. BO all sts kwise on next row.

Neckband

With smaller 16" (40 cm) cir needle, RS facing, and beg at outer edge of right placket, pick up and knit 25 (27, 27, 29, 29) sts evenly spaced along right front edge, 38 (40, 40, 42, 42) sts across back neck, and 25 (27, 27, 29, 29) sts along left front edge, ending at end of left placket—88 (94, 94, 100, 100) sts total. Knit 2 rows. BO all sts kwise.

Short Ties (make 2)

With crochet hook and leaving a tail about 6" (15 cm) long, make a ch (see Glossary for crochet instructions) about 12 (12, 12¾, 13½, 14)" (30.5 [30.5, 32.5, 34.5, 35.5] cm) long. Beg with second ch from hook, work sl st in each ch to end of ch. Fasten off, leaving a tail about 6" (15 cm) long. With tails threaded on a tapestry needle, secure one tie to the WS of each front, near the center front eyelet on the body. Bring the free end of tie to the front through the eyelet.

The neckband is easy—pick up stitches, knit two rows, and bind off!

Long Tie

With crochet hook, make a ch about 46 (48, 51, 54, 57)" (117 [122, 129.5, 137, 145] cm) long. Beg with second ch from hook, work sl st in each ch to end of ch. Fasten off. Weave in tails to ends of tie.

With yarn threaded on a tapestry needle, sew sleeves into armholes. Sew buttons to left front opposite buttonholes. Beg and end on RS, thread long tie through rem eyelets.

Change needle size
to create flair in the
lower body

For this A-line skirt, Kat Coyle took inspiration from a Guernsey sweater in Gladys Thompson's *Patterns for Guernseys, Jerseys & Arans: Fishermen's Sweaters from the British Isles* (Dover, 1979). Kat's skirt is worked in the round from the hem up, starting with a garter-stitch border that's followed by a wide section of stockinette stitch, just like a traditional Guernsey pullover. The upper half of the skirt is decorated with a richly textured combination of cables, ribs, ladder stitch, and moss stitch. To taper the circumference from the hips to the waist, Kat worked paired decreases in the ribbed section along the side "seams." A ribbed casing for elastic at the waistband allows for a customized fit.

STITCH GUIDE

Garter Stitch in Rounds
Rnd 1: Knit.
Rnd 2: Purl.
Repeat Rnds 1 and 2 for pattern.

NOTES

✤ Choose your size with a bit of negative ease in the hips—the ribbed stitches at the sides will provide the necessary give.

✤ To facilitate sewing the waistband, run smooth waste yarn through the first round of waistband stitches before working them. Use this yarn as a guide when securing the live stitches of the facing.

FINISHED SIZE
About 30½ (35½, 40¾)" (77.5 [90, 103.5] cm) waist circumference without elastic and 34¾ (38, 43¼)" (88.5 [96.5, 110] cm) hip circumference, measured 5¾" (14.5 cm) below waistband. Skirt shown measures 34¾" (88.5 cm) at hips.

YARN
Worsted weight (#4 Medium).
Shown here: Black Water Abbey Yarns 2-Ply Worsted Weight (100% wool; 220 yd [201 m]/4 oz): rust, 4 (4, 5) skeins.

NEEDLES
Size U.S. 7 (4.5 mm): 24" (60 cm) circular (cir). Size U.S. 6 (4 mm): 24" (60 cm) cir. Adjust needle size if necessary to obtain the correct gauge.

NOTIONS
Markers (m); cable needle (cn); tapestry needle; waste yarn (optional; see Notes); ¾" (2 cm) nonrolling waistband elastic to measure 1" (2.5 cm) less than actual waist measurement; sharp-point sewing needle; matching sewing thread.

GAUGE
18 stitches and 26 rounds = 4" (10 cm) in stockinette stitch on larger needle worked in the round, after blocking.

Cable and Moss

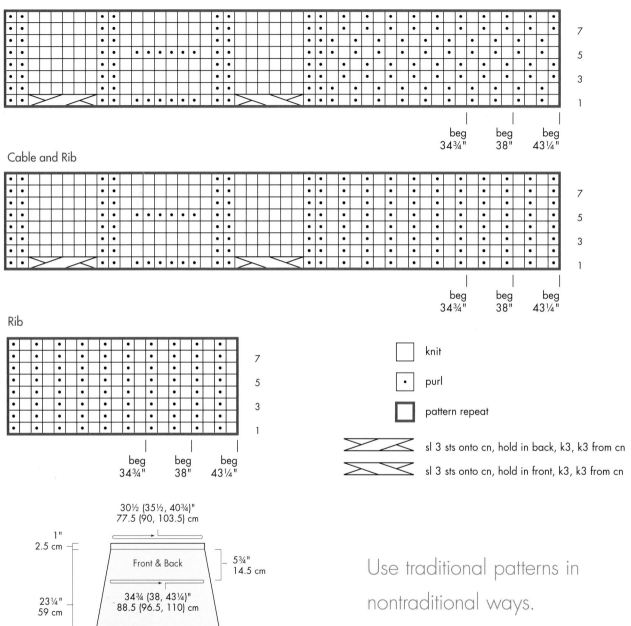

7

5

3

1

beg
34¾"

beg
38"

beg
43¼"

Cable and Rib

7

5

3

1

beg
34¾"

beg
38"

beg
43¼"

Rib

7

5

3

1

beg
34¾"

beg
38"

beg
43¼"

knit

• purl

pattern repeat

sl 3 sts onto cn, hold in back, k3, k3 from cn

sl 3 sts onto cn, hold in front, k3, k3 from cn

30½ (35½, 40¾)"
77.5 (90, 103.5) cm

1"
2.5 cm

Front & Back

5¾"
14.5 cm

34¾ (38, 43¼)"
88.5 (96.5, 110) cm

23¼"
59 cm

48 (53¼, 58¾)"
122 (135.5, 149) cm

Use traditional patterns in
nontraditional ways.

SKIRT

With larger needle, CO 216 (240, 264) sts. Place marker (pm) and join for working in rnds, being careful not to twist sts. Work 6 rnds in garter st (see Stitch Guide). Change to St st (knit all rnds). *Next rnd:* K108 (120, 132), pm, knit to end. Work 3 rnds even. *Dec rnd:* *K1, ssk (see Glossary), knit to 3 sts before next m, k2tog, k1, slip marker (sl m); rep from *—4 sts dec'd. Dec 2 sts at each marker in this manner every 10th rnd 4 more times, then every 8th rnd 2 times—188 (212, 236) sts rem. Knit 5 rnds—piece measures about 11" (28 cm) from CO. Purl 2 rnds. *Dec rnd:* *K1, ssk, knit to 3 sts before next m, k2tog, k1, sl m; rep from *—184 (208, 232) sts rem. Knit 1 rnd. Purl 2 rnds. Beg as indicated for your hip size, *work 40 (44, 48) sts according to Cable and Rib chart, work 40 (44, 48) sts according to Cable and Moss chart, work 12 (16, 20) sts according to Rib chart; rep from * once more. Cont as established, work chart Rows 1–8 a total of 9 times, then work Rows 1 and 2 once more and *at the same time* dec 4 sts on 9th rnd, then dec 4 sts every 8th rnd 8 more times, working dec rnd as foll: *P1, ssk, work in patt to 3 sts before m, k2tog, p1; rep from * once more—148 (172, 196) sts rem.

Waistband

Work in k1, p1 rib for 1" (2.5 cm; see Notes). Purl 1 rnd. Change to smaller cir needle and work in St st for 1" (2.5 cm) for facing. Do not BO. Cut yarn, leaving a tail about 92 (107, 122)" (233.5 [272, 310] cm) long.

FINISHING

Cut waistband elastic to 1" (2.5 cm) shorter than actual waist measurement. With sewing needle and thread, sew ends of elastic together to form a ring. Place ring inside waistband, fold facing to WS, and with long tail threaded on a tapestry needle, sew live sts to WS of first row of ribbing. Weave in loose ends. Wet block to measurements, opening up cable sections.

Véronik Avery chose a circular construction for this striking asymmetric cardigan. The body is knitted in a single piece from the hem to the armholes, the sleeves (worked upward from the cuffs) are added, then the yoke is worked to the top of the foldover collar. Decorative mirrored decreases border a couple of reverse stockinette stitches to produce an unusual textural pattern along the four raglan lines that resembles cables. A wide knit-two-purl-two rib along the hem, cuffs, and front opening provides just the right amount of visual interest to an otherwise plain sweater. Rather than fuss with buttons and buttonhole placement, Véronik chose to fasten the cardigan with large hook-and-eye closures.

STITCH GUIDE

Right-Leaning Double Decrease
Slip 2 sts onto cn and hold cn parallel to and behind left needle. *Insert right needle into first st on left needle and first st on cn, knit these 2 sts tog; rep from * once—2 sts dec'd.

Left-Leaning Double Decrease
Slip 2 sts onto cn and hold cn parallel to and in front of left needle. *Insert right needle into first st on cn and first st on left needle, knit these 2 sts tog; rep from * once—2 sts dec'd.

LOWER BODY

With cir needle, CO 174 (190, 206, 222, 238, 254, 270) sts. Do not join. *Set-up rib:* (RS) *K2, p2; rep from * to last 2 sts, k2. Cont in rib as established (knit the knits and purl the purls) until piece measures 3 (3, 3¼, 3¼, 3½, 3½, 3¾)" (7.5 [7.5, 8.5, 8.5, 9, 9, 9.5] cm) from CO. Work even in St st (knit RS rows; purl WS rows) until piece measures 13¾ (14, 14¼, 14½, 14¾, 15, 15¼)" (35 [35.5, 36, 37, 37.5, 38, 38.5] cm) from CO, ending with a WS row.

Divide for Fronts and Back
(RS) K46 (50, 55, 60, 64, 67, 73) right front sts, BO 8 (8, 10, 12, 12, 14, 14) sts for right armhole, k84 (92, 98, 104, 112, 118, 126) back sts, BO 8 (8, 10, 12, 12, 14, 14) sts for left armhole, k28 (32, 33, 34, 38, 41, 43) left front sts. Do not cut yarn. Set aside.

FINISHED SIZE
About 37 (40, 43, 46½, 49½, 53, 56)" (94 [101.5, 109, 118, 125.5, 134.5, 142] cm) bust circumference, fastened. Sweater shown measures 40" (101.5 cm).

YARN
Worsted weight (#4 Medium).

Shown here: Brown Sheep Lamb's Pride Worsted (85% wool, 15% mohair; 190 yd [174 m]/113 g): M184 pistachio, 6 (7, 8, 9, 9, 10, 11) skeins.

NEEDLES
Size U.S. 6 (4 mm): 32" (80 cm) circular (cir) and set of 4 or 5 double-pointed (dpn). Adjust needle size if necessary to obtain the correct gauge.

NOTIONS
Markers (m); cable needle (cn); tapestry needle; four ¾" (2 cm) hook-and-eye closures (available at fabric stores).

GAUGE
20 stitches and 30 rows = 4" (10 cm) in stockinette stitch.

SLEEVES

With dpn, CO 48 (52, 56, 60, 60, 64, 64) sts. Divide sts evenly onto 3 or 4 dpn, place marker (pm), and join for working in rnds, being careful not to twists sts. Work in k2, p2 rib until piece measures 3 (3, 3¼, 3¼, 3½, 3½, 3¾)" (7.5 [7.5, 8.5, 8.5, 9, 9, 9.5] cm) from CO. Work even in St st until piece measures 5¼ (5¾, 5, 4, 4¾, 4¼, 6½)" (13.5 [14.5, 12.5, 10, 12, 11, 16.5] cm) from CO. *Inc rnd:* K1, M1 (see Glossary), knit to last st, M1, k1—2 sts inc'd. Work 9 (9, 9, 9, 7, 7, 5) rnds even. Rep the last 10 (10, 10, 10, 8, 8, 6) rnds 6 (6, 7, 8, 10, 11, 13) more times—62 (66, 72, 78, 82, 88, 92) sts. Work even until piece measures 16 (16½, 17, 17¾, 18¼, 18¾, 19¼)" (40.5 [42, 43, 45, 46.5, 47.5, 49] cm) from CO, ending last rnd 4 (4, 5, 6, 6, 7, 7) sts before marker. BO 8 (8, 10, 12, 12, 14, 14) sts, knit to end—54 (58, 62, 66, 70, 74, 78) sts rem. Cut yarn.

Substitute hook-and-eye closures for buttons and buttonholes.

YOKE

With WS facing and yarn attached to body, p27 (31, 32, 33, 37, 40, 42) left front sts, k1 left front st, pm, k1 left sleeve st, p52 (56, 60, 64, 68, 72, 76) left sleeve sts, k1 left sleeve st, pm, k1 back st, p82 (90, 96, 102, 110, 116, 124) back sts, k1 back st, pm, k1 right sleeve st, p52 (56, 60, 64, 68, 72, 76) right sleeve sts, k1 right sleeve st, pm, k1 right front st, p45 (49, 54, 59, 63, 66, 72) right front sts—266 (290, 310, 330, 354, 374, 398) sts total. Work 2 rows as established (knit the knits and purl the purls). *Dec row:* *Knit to 5 sts before m, work left-leaning double decrease (see Stitch Guide), p1, slip marker (sl m), p1, work right-leaning double decrease (see Stitch Guide); rep from * 3 more times, knit to end—16 sts dec'd. Work 3 rows even as established. Rep the last 4 rows 11 (12, 13, 14, 15, 16, 17) more times—74 (82, 86, 90, 98, 102, 110) sts rem. Work 1 row, dec 2 sts evenly spaced—72 (80, 84, 88, 96, 100, 108) sts rem.

Collar

(WS) P3, *k2, p2; rep from * to last 5 sts, k2, p3. Work even in rib as established for 4¼ (4¼, 4¼, 4¾, 4¾, 4¾, 5)" (11 [11, 11, 12, 12, 12, 12.5] cm). BO all sts in patt.

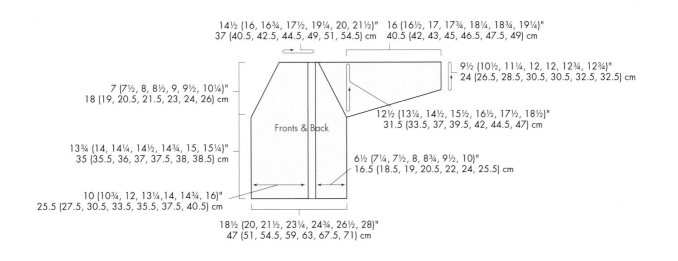

14½ (16, 16¾, 17½, 19¼, 20, 21½)"
37 (40.5, 42.5, 44.5, 49, 51, 54.5) cm

16 (16½, 17, 17¾, 18¼, 18¾, 19¼)"
40.5 (42, 43, 45, 46.5, 47.5, 49) cm

9½ (10½, 11¼, 12, 12, 12¾, 12¾)"
24 (26.5, 28.5, 30.5, 30.5, 32.5, 32.5) cm

7 (7½, 8, 8½, 9, 9½, 10¼)"
18 (19, 20.5, 21.5, 23, 24, 26) cm

12½ (13¼, 14½, 15½, 16½, 17½, 18½)"
31.5 (33.5, 37, 39.5, 42, 44.5, 47) cm

Fronts & Back

13¾ (14, 14¼, 14½, 14¾, 15, 15¼)"
35 (35.5, 36, 37, 37.5, 38, 38.5) cm

6½ (7¼, 7½, 8, 8¾, 9½, 10)"
16.5 (18.5, 19, 20.5, 22, 24, 25.5) cm

10 (10¾, 12, 13¼, 14, 14¾, 16)"
25.5 (27.5, 30.5, 33.5, 35.5, 37.5, 40.5) cm

18½ (20, 21½, 23¼, 24¾, 26½, 28)"
47 (51, 54.5, 59, 63, 67.5, 71) cm

FINISHING

Weave in loose ends.

Right Front Band

With cir needle, RS facing, and beg at lower right front edge, pick up and knit 124 (128, 132, 140, 144, 148, 152) sts evenly spaced along right front, ending at top of collar. Knit 1 WS row. *Next row:* (RS) K4, *p2, k2; rep from *. *Next row:* (WS) K4, *p2, k2; rep from * to end. Maintaining first 2 and last 2 sts in garter st (knit every row), work even as established until band measures 3" (7.5 cm) from pick-up row, ending with a WS row. With RS facing, BO all sts in patt.

Left Front Band

With cir needle, RS facing, and beg at top of left front collar, pick up and knit 124 (128, 132, 140, 144, 148, 152) sts evenly spaced along left front. Knit 1 WS row. *Next row:* (RS) K2, *p2, k2; rep from * to last 2 sts, k2. *Next row:* (WS) *K2, p2; rep from * to last 4 sts, k4. Complete as for right front band.

With yarn threaded on a tapestry needle, sew underarm seams. Mark placement for 4 hook-and-eye closures on front bands, placing the first at base of collar, the last about 3½" (9 cm) below underarm, and the others evenly spaced in between. Sew hooks to RS of left front band and eyes to WS of right front band. Block to finished measurements.

Work the ribbing on the same needles as the body to reduce draw-in.

Katie Himmelberg's jumper couldn't be simpler—it's worked entirely without seams and requires no additional edging. Katie cast on stitches for the bodice and worked a body-hugging rib to the waist, then changed to stockinette stitch for the skirt, which she shaped with four sets of subtle paired increases. A few rounds of garter stitch at the hem prevent the fabric from curling. For the straps, Katie picked up stitches at the top of the bodice back and worked them in a sturdy knit-one-purl-one rib, adding a buttonhole at the end. She tried on the jumper to determine the best button placement, sewed on the buttons, and she was done. Lovely.

BODICE

With smaller needle, CO 135 (150, 165, 180, 195) sts. Place marker (pm) and join for working in rnds, being careful not to twist sts. *Set-up rnd:* *K3, p2; rep from *. Cont in rib as established until piece measures 9¾ (10, 10¼, 10½, 10¾)" (25 [25.5, 26, 26.5, 27.5] cm) from CO. *Next rnd:* *K3, p1, M1 pwise (see Glossary), p1; rep from *—162 (180, 198, 216, 234) sts.

SKIRT

Change to larger needle. Work even in St st (knit all rnds) for 1¾" (4.5 cm). *Inc rnd:* K20 (22, 24, 27, 29), M1R (see Glossary), k1 and mark the st with a removable marker, M1L (see Glossary), k40 (44, 49, 53, 57), M1R, k1 and mark this st, M1L, k39 (44, 48, 53, 58), M1R, k1 and mark this st, M1L, k40 (44, 49, 53, 57), M1R, k1 and mark this st, M1L, k19 (22, 24, 26, 29)—8 sts inc'd. Knit 7 rnds. *Inc rnd:* *Knit to marked st, M1R, k1, M1L; rep from * 3 more times, knit to end of rnd—8 sts inc'd. Rep the last 8 rnds 12 more times, moving markers up every few rnds—274 (292, 310, 328, 346) sts. [Purl 1 rnd, knit 1 rnd] 3 times, purl 1 rnd. Loosely BO all sts kwise.

FINISHED SIZE

21½ (24, 26½, 28¾, 31¼)" (54.5 [61, 67.5, 73, 79.5] cm) bust circumference with rib relaxed. To fit bust size 32–34, 35–37, 38–40, 40–42, 43–45)" (81.5–86.5 [89–94, 96.5–101.5, 101.5–106.5, 109–114.5] cm). Jumper shown measures 21½" (54.5 cm).

YARN

Worsted weight (#4 Medium).

Shown here: Berroco Ultra Alpaca (50% super fine alpaca, 50% Peruvian highland wool; 215 yd [197 m]/100 g): #6294 turquoise mix, 4 (5, 6, 6, 6) skeins.

NEEDLES

Bodice—size U.S. 7 (4.5 mm): 24" (60 cm) circular (cir). Skirt—size U.S. 8 (5 mm): 24" (60 cm) cir. Adjust needle size if necessary to obtain the correct gauge.

NOTIONS

Marker (m); removable markers or safety pins; tapestry needle; two 1½" (3.8 cm) buttons.

GAUGE

20 stitches and 28 rounds = 4" (10 cm) in stockinette stitch on larger needle, worked in rounds.

Ribbing provides
a close, flexible fit
in the bodice.

STRAPS

Mark bodice center back. Count 10 sts to each side of center and mark next st for strap placements.

Right Strap

With smaller needle, RS facing, and beg 11 (11, 11, 13, 13) sts to the right of the right strap marker, pick up and knit 11 (11, 11, 13, 13) sts. *Set-up row:* (WS) *P1, k1; rep from * to last st, p1. Cont in rib as established (knit the knits and purl the purls) until strap measures about 13" (33 cm), ending with a WS row. *Split for buttonhole:* Keeping in patt, work 5 (5, 5, 6, 6) sts, join second ball of yarn and k2tog (k2tog, k2tog, p2tog, p2tog), then work in rib to end—5 (5, 5, 6, 6) sts each side. Work each side separately in patt until buttonhole slit measures 1" (2.5 cm), ending with a WS row. *Joining row:* (RS) Keeping in patt, work 5 (5, 5, 6, 6) sts, using same yarn p1f&b (p1f&b, p1f&b, k1f&b, k1f&b) (see Glossary), work to end—11 (11, 11, 13, 13) sts. Work in patt for 1" (2.5 cm) more. BO as foll: Sl 1, *k2tog, pass previous st over; rep from * to end.

Left Strap

With smaller needle, RS facing, and beg at the left strap marker, pick up and knit 11 (11, 11, 13, 13) sts. Work as for right strap.

FINISHING

Weave in loose ends. Block to measurements. Try on jumper and mark desired placement for buttons. With yarn threaded on a tapestry needle, sew buttons to bodice front.

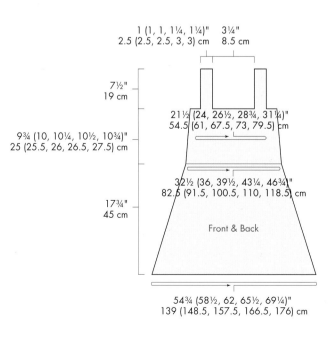

1 (1, 1, 1¼, 1¼)"   3¼"
2.5 (2.5, 2.5, 3, 3) cm   8.5 cm

7½"
19 cm

21½ (24, 26½, 28¾, 31¼)"
54.5 (61, 67.5, 73, 79.5) cm

9¾ (10, 10¼, 10½, 10¾)"
25 (25.5, 26, 26.5, 27.5) cm

32½ (36, 39½, 43¼, 46¾)"
82.5 (91.5, 100.5, 110, 118.5) cm

17¾"
45 cm

Front & Back

54¾ (58½, 62, 65½, 69¼)"
139 (148.5, 157.5, 166.5, 176) cm

Talk about simple—
there's no edging or
seaming involved in
this jumper!

Ann E. Smith combined simple texture with simple colorwork in this warm and comfy pullover. She worked the lower body, sleeves, and neckband in a modified rib pattern that involves purling all stitches on all wrong-side rows, and she worked the upper body in a stranded Fair Isle pattern that never has more than two colors in the same row. She added textural interest to the dot pattern by working the dots in a two-row sequence— knitted on the first row, purled on the second. To eliminate all but a small seam at each underarm, Ann picked up stitches around the modified drop-shoulder shaping and worked the sleeves in the round to the cuffs.

STITCH GUIDE

Rib Pattern (multiple of 2 sts + 1)
Row 1: (RS) K1, *p1, k1; rep from *.
Row 2: (WS) Purl.
Rep Rows 1 and 2 for pattern.

Bumps Pattern (multiple of 6 sts + 5 [7, 9, 7])
Row 1: (RS) K2 (3, 4, 3) with CC1, *k1 with CC2, k5 with CC1; rep from * to last 3 (4, 5, 4) sts, k1 with CC2, k2 (3, 4, 3) with CC1.
Row 2: (WS) P2 (3, 4, 3) with CC1, *k1 with CC2, p5 with CC1; rep from * to last 3 (4, 5, 4) sts, k1 with CC2, p2 (3, 4, 3) with CC1.

BACK

With MC, CO 71 (79, 87, 97) sts. Beg with Row 1, work rib patt (see Stitch Guide) until piece measures 10" (25.5 cm) from CO, ending with a WS row. Beg and end as indicated for your size, work Rows 1–14 of Fair Isle chart. With CC1, work 2 rows in St st. Work 2-row bumps patt (see Stitch Guide). With CC1, work 6 rows in St st. Rep the last 8 rows for patt and *at the same time* when piece measures 15" (38 cm) from CO, ending with a WS row, shape armholes as foll.

Shape Armholes

Keeping in patt, BO 9 (11, 13, 16) sts at beg of next 2 rows—53 (57, 61, 65) sts rem. Cont in patt until armholes measure 8 (8½, 9, 9½)" (20.5 [21.5, 23, 24] cm), ending with a WS row. BO all sts.

FINISHED SIZE
About 38 (42, 46½, 51½)" (96.5 [106.5, 118, 131] cm) bust circumference. Pullover shown measures 38" (96.5 cm).

YARN
Chunky weight (#5 Bulky).
Shown here: Nashua Handknits Creative Focus Chunky (75% wool, 25% alpaca; 110 yd [101 m]/100 g): #CFC1450 blue pine (MC), 7 (7, 8, 9) balls; #CFC1117 grass (CC1), 2 (3, 3, 4) balls; #CFC3729 rust (CC2), 1 ball (all sizes).

NEEDLES
Size U.S. 10 (6 mm): straight and 16" (40 cm) circular (cir). Adjust needle size if necessary to obtain the correct gauge.

NOTIONS
Tapestry needle; marker (m); removable markers.

GAUGE
15 stitches and 18 rows = 4" (10 cm) in stockinette stitch.

Keep colorwork patterns simple by working only two colors per row.

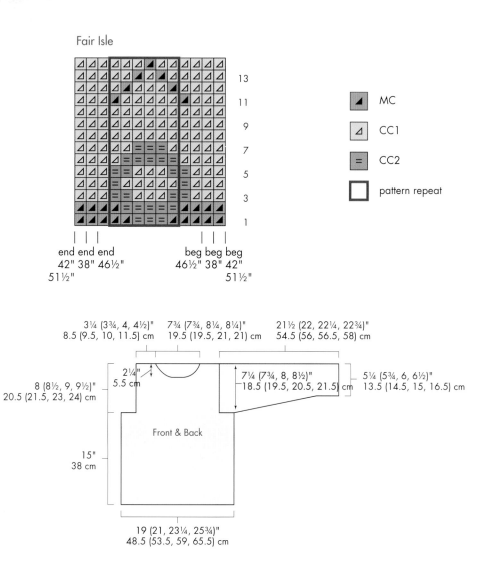

Fair Isle

	MC
	CC1
	CC2
	pattern repeat

FRONT

Work as for back until armholes measure 5¾ (6¼, 6¾, 7¼)" (14.5 [16, 17, 18.5] cm), ending with a WS row—53 (57, 61, 65) sts.

Shape Neck

(RS) Cont in patt, work 18 (20, 21, 23) sts, join a second ball of yarn and BO center 17 (17, 19, 19) sts for neck, work to end—18 (20, 21, 23) sts rem each side. Working each side separately, at each neck edge BO 3 sts once, then BO 2 sts once, then BO 1 st once—12 (14, 15, 17) sts rem. Cont even until piece measures same as back, ending with a WS row. BO all sts.

SLEEVES

With CC1 threaded on a tapestry needle, sew front to back at shoulders. With MC, RS facing, and beg and ending at end of the armhole BO sts, pick up and knit 55 (59, 61, 65) sts evenly spaced along the straight edge of the armhole. Beg with Row 2, work rib patt for 13 (15, 17,

19) rows. Place a removable marker at each end of last row. *Dec row:* Keeping in patt, dec 1 st each end of needle—2 sts dec'd. Work 5 rows even. Rep the last 6 rows 7 more times—39 (43, 45, 49) sts rem. Work even in patt until piece measures 21½ (22, 22¼, 22¾)" (54.5 [56, 56.5, 58] cm) from pick-up row, ending with a WS row. BO all sts in patt.

FINISHING

Block to measurements. Weave in loose ends. With MC threaded on a tapestry needle, sew sleeve and underarm seams, matching sleeve markers to beg of BO sts of armhole. Sew side seams.

Neckband

With CC1, cir needle, RS facing, and beg at right shoulder seam, pick up and knit 29 (29, 31, 31) sts across back neck, 13 sts along left front neck, 17 (17, 19, 19) sts across center front neck, and 13 sts along right front neck—72 (72, 76, 76) sts total. Place marker (pm) and join for working in rnds.

Rnd 1: Purl.
Rnd 2: Change to MC. Knit.
Rnd 3: *K1, p1; rep from *.
Rnds 4–11: Rep Rnds 2 and 3 four times.
Rnd 12: Knit.
BO all sts in patt.

Modified drop-shoulder
shaping is easy to knit
and easy to seam.

Have you ever artfully draped a shawl around your shoulders only to have it fall down as soon as you moved your arms? In this sleeved version, Mags Kandis has come up with a clever way to allow full arm movement while keeping the wrap in place. Mags knitted a long seed-stitch rectangle accented with a braided cable along one edge, and added slits for armholes along the way. Then she picked up stitches around the slits and knitted the sleeves downward to the cuffs—voilà! A wrap that stays put. Worked without any shaping or finishing details, this piece knits up in a jiffy.

STITCH GUIDE

Seed Stitch (multiple of 2 sts + 1)
Row/Rnd 1: K1, *p1, k1; rep from *.
Row/Rnd 2: Work the sts opposite of how they appear (purl the knits and knit the purls). Rep these 2 rows/rounds for pattern.

NOTES

✤ This piece is worked from side to side.

✤ For a tidy edge, join new balls of yarn 3 stitches in from right edge with the right side facing.

BODY

With straight needles, CO 60 (60, 64, 68) sts. *Set-up row:* (RS) Work 3 sts in seed st (see Stitch Guide), work next 22 sts according to Row 1 of Cable chart, work rem 35 (35, 39, 43) sts in seed st. Cont as established until piece measures about 11¾ (11¾, 12¾, 14)" (30 [30, 32.5, 35.5] cm) from CO, ending with a WS row.

FINISHED SIZE
About 10½ (11½, 12½, 13½)" (26.5 [29, 31.5, 34.5] cm) back width between armholes. Wrap shown measures 11½" (29 cm) across back.

YARN
Worsted weight (#4 Medium).

Shown here: Blue Sky Alpacas Worsted Hand Dyes (50% alpaca, 50% merino; 100 yd [91 m]/100 g): #2010 rusty orange, 10 (10, 12, 13) balls.

NEEDLES
Size U.S. 10 (6 mm): straight and 12" (30 cm) circular or set of 4 or 5 double-pointed (dpn). Adjust needle size if necessary to obtain the correct gauge.

NOTIONS
Cable needle (cn); marker (m); tapestry needle.

GAUGE
13 stitches and 23 rows or rounds = 4" (10 cm) in seed stitch.

Knit a rectangle with sleeves
for a wrap that stays put.

Cable

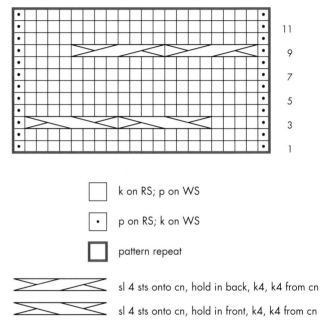

11
9
7
5
3
1

☐ k on RS; p on WS

• p on RS; k on WS

☐ pattern repeat

sl 4 sts onto cn, hold in back, k4, k4 from cn

sl 4 sts onto cn, hold in front, k4, k4 from cn

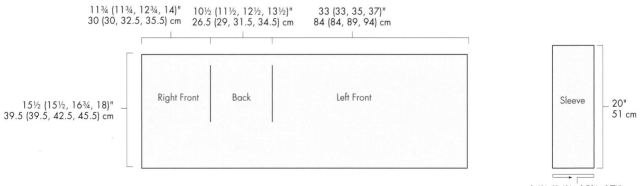

11¾ (11¾, 12¾, 14)"
30 (30, 32.5, 35.5) cm

10½ (11½, 12½, 13½)"
26.5 (29, 31.5, 34.5) cm

33 (33, 35, 37)"
84 (84, 89, 94) cm

15½ (15½, 16¾, 18)"
39.5 (39.5, 42.5, 45.5) cm

Right Front

Back

Left Front

Sleeve

20"
51 cm

14½ (14½, 15¾, 17)"
37 (37, 40, 43) cm

Right Armhole

Keeping in patt as established, work 26 sts, BO next 22 (22, 24, 26) sts for armhole, work to end. *Next row:* Work 12 (12, 14, 16) sts, use the backward-loop method (see Glossary) to CO 22 (22, 24, 26) sts over gap formed on previous row, work to end. Work even in patt until piece measures about 10½ (11½, 12½, 13½)" (26.5 [29, 31.5, 34.5] cm) from right armhole, ending with a WS row.

Left Armhole

Keeping in patt, work 26 sts, BO next 22 (22, 24, 26) sts for armhole, work to end. *Next row:* Work 12 (12, 14, 16) sts, use the backward-loop method to CO 22 (22, 24, 26) sts over gap, work to end. Work even in patt until piece measures about 33 (33, 35, 37)" (84 [84, 89, 94] cm) from left armhole, ending with a WS row. With RS facing, BO all sts in patt.

SLEEVES

With cir needle or dpn and RS facing, pick up and knit 22 (22, 24, 26) sts evenly spaced along CO edge of armhole opening, 2 sts at corner, 22 (22, 24, 26) sts along BO edge of armhole opening, and 1 st at other corner—47 (47, 51, 55) sts total. Place marker (pm) and join for working in rnds. Work in seed st in rnds (see Stitch Guide) until piece measures about 20" (51 cm) from pick-up rnd, or desired total length. BO all sts in patt.

FINISHING

Weave in loose ends. Block lightly to measurements.

Did you knit a stiff garter-stitch scarf for your first project and then immediately move on to other stitches? For this Chanel-inspired jacket, Ann Budd revisited the most basic of stitches. She paired it with a soft wool-bamboo yarn and worked it at a looser gauge than suggested on the ball band to produce a fabric with exquisite drape. She worked the back and sleeves from the bottom up in the usual manner, but she worked the fronts sideways from the scalloped lace pattern to the side seams, with the neck and armholes shaped along the way. The edging on the neck and hem looks like I-cord but is much easier to work—simply pick up stitches, knit a row, then bind off!

BACK

CO 85 (95, 105, 115) sts. Beg with a WS row, work even in garter st (knit every row) until piece measures 13½ (14, 15¼, 16)" (34.5 [35.5, 38.5, 40.5] cm) from CO, ending with a WS row.

Shape Armholes

BO 5 sts at beg of next 2 rows—75 (85, 95, 105) sts rem. Dec 1 st each end of needle every RS row 4 (5, 8, 10) times—67 (75, 79, 85) sts rem. Work even until armhole measures 7 (7½, 8, 8½)" (18 [19, 20.5, 21.5] cm), ending with a WS row. BO all sts.

RIGHT FRONT

CO 93 (93, 93, 111) sts. *Set-up row:* (WS) K1 (selvedge st; knit every row), work 91 (91, 91, 109) sts according to set-up row of Lace and Rib chart, k1 (selvedge st; knit every row). Knitting the first and last st of every row, work Rows 1–20 of chart. Knit 2 rows, ending with a WS row.

Shape Neck

With RS facing, use the cable method (see Glossary) to CO 9 (15, 23, 11) sts at beg of row, then knit these 9 (15, 23, 11) sts, then knit to end of row—102 (108, 116, 122) sts. Work even in garter st until piece measures 3½ (4¼, 4½, 4¾)" (9 [11, 11.5, 12] cm) from neck CO, ending with a WS row.

FINISHED SIZE
About 34 (38, 42, 46)" (86.5 [96.5, 106.5, 117] cm) bust circumference, including a ½ (1½, 1, 1½)" (1.3 [3.8, 2.5, 3.8] cm) gap at center front. Sweater shown measures 38" (96.5 cm).

YARN
DK weight (#3 Light).

Shown here: Classic Elite Wool Bam Boo (50% wool, 50% bamboo; 118 yd [108 m]/50 g): #1689 watermelon, 10 (11, 13, 14) balls.

NEEDLES
Size U.S. 8 (5 mm). Adjust needle size if necessary to obtain the correct gauge.

NOTIONS
Tapestry needle.

GAUGE
20 stitches and 38 rows = 4" (10 cm) in garter stitch.

Lace and Rib

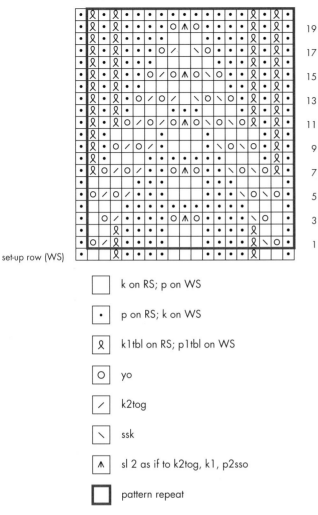

set-up row (WS)

Chart row numbers (right side): 19, 17, 15, 13, 11, 9, 7, 5, 3, 1

Legend

(blank)	k on RS; p on WS
•	p on RS; k on WS
ℚ	k1tbl on RS; p1tbl on WS
O	yo
/	k2tog
\	ssk
ʌ	sl 2 as if to k2tog, k1, p2sso
(box outline)	pattern repeat

Shape Armhole

With RS facing, BO 30 (30, 32, 32) sts, knit to end—72 (78, 84, 90) sts rem. BO 1 (3, 1, 1) st(s) at beg of next 4 (2, 8, 10) RS rows, then BO 0 (2, 0, 0) sts at beg of foll RS row—68 (70, 76, 80) sts rem. Work even in garter st until piece measures 1" (2.5 cm) from last BO row, ending with a WS row. With RS facing, BO all sts.

LEFT FRONT

CO 93 (93, 93, 111) sts. *Set-up row:* (WS) K1 (selvedge st; knit every row), work 91 (91, 91, 109) sts according to set-up row of Lace and Rib chart, k1 (selvedge st; knit every row). Knitting the first and last st of every row, work Rows 1–20 of chart. Knit 1 row, ending with a RS row.

Shape Neck

With WS facing, use the cable method to CO 9 (15, 23, 11) sts at beg of row, then knit these 9 (15, 23, 11) sts, then knit to end of row—102 (108, 116, 122) sts. Work even in garter st until piece measures 3½ (4¼, 4½, 4¾)" (9 [11, 11.5, 12] cm) from neck CO, ending with a RS row.

Shape Armhole

With WS facing, BO 30 (30, 32, 32) sts, knit to end—72 (78, 84, 90) sts rem. BO 1 (3, 1, 1) st(s) at beg of next 4 (2, 8, 10) WS rows, then BO 0 (2, 0, 0) sts at beg of foll WS row—68 (70, 76, 80) sts rem. Work even in garter st until piece measures 1" (2.5 cm) from last BO row, ending with a RS row. With WS facing, BO all sts.

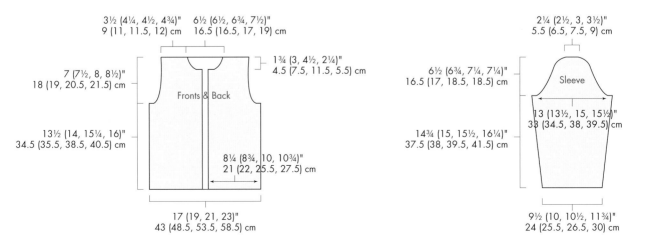

3½ (4¼, 4½, 4¾)"
9 (11, 11.5, 12) cm

6½ (6½, 6¾, 7½)"
16.5 (16.5, 17, 19) cm

1¾ (3, 4½, 2¼)"
4.5 (7.5, 11.5, 5.5) cm

7 (7½, 8, 8½)"
18 (19, 20.5, 21.5) cm

Fronts & Back

13½ (14, 15¼, 16)"
34.5 (35.5, 38.5, 40.5) cm

8¼ (8¾, 10, 10¾)"
21 (22, 25.5, 27.5) cm

17 (19, 21, 23)"
43 (48.5, 53.5, 58.5) cm

2¼ (2½, 3, 3½)"
5.5 (6.5, 7.5, 9) cm

6½ (6¾, 7¼, 7¼)"
16.5 (17, 18.5, 18.5) cm

Sleeve

13 (13½, 15, 15½)"
33 (34.5, 38, 39.5) cm

14¾ (15, 15½, 16¼)"
37.5 (38, 39.5, 41.5) cm

9½ (10, 10½, 11¾)"
24 (25.5, 26.5, 30) cm

SLEEVES

CO 47 (50, 53, 59) sts. Beg with a WS row, work even in garter st until piece measures 2"
(5 cm) from CO, ending with a WS row. Inc 1 st each end of needle on next (RS) row, then every 12 (12, 10, 14)th row 8 (8, 10, 8) more times—65 (68, 75, 77) sts. Work even until piece measures 14¾ (15, 15½, 16¼)" (37.5 [38, 39.5, 41.5] cm) from CO, ending with a WS row.

Shape Cap

BO 4 sts at beg of next 2 rows—57 (60, 67, 69) sts rem. Dec 1 st each end of needle every RS row 4 (5, 6, 6) times—49 (50, 55, 57) sts rem. Dec 1 st each end of needle every 4th row 11 (11, 12, 12) times—27 (28, 31, 33) sts rem. BO 2 sts at beg of next 8 rows—11 (12, 15, 17) sts rem. BO all sts.

FINISHING

Block pieces to measurements. Weave in loose ends. With yarn threaded on a tapestry needle, sew fronts to back at shoulders. Sew sleeve caps into armholes, centering the BO row of the caps at the shoulder seams. Sew sleeve and side seams.

Neck Edging

With RS facing and beg at upper right center front, pick up and knit 16 sts across lace panel, 10 (16, 23, 12) sts to shoulder seam, 36 (36, 37, 41) sts across back neck to other shoulder seam, 10 (16, 23, 12) sts along left front, and 16 sts across lace panel—88 (100, 115, 97) sts total. Knit 1 row. BO all sts.

Lower Edging

With RS facing and beg at lower left center front, pick up and knit 16 sts across lace panel, 27 (29, 35, 39) sts to side seam, 83 (93, 103, 113) sts across back to other side seam, 27 (29, 35, 39) sts to right front lace panel, and 16 sts across lace panel—169 (183, 205, 223) sts total. Knit 1 row. BO all sts.

Block again if desired.

Don't overlook the simple
beauty of garter stitch.

Worked with big yarn and big needles, Therese Chynoweth's short vest is a true "quick knit." She worked the body in the round to the armholes, beginning with a few inches of knit-one-purl-one rib at the hem. She then divided the fronts and back at the armholes and worked them separately to the shoulders, incorporating simple ribbed edges at the neck and armholes along the way. The double-cable panel on the front grows out of the ribbing, then it splits at the base of the neck, and one cable borders each side of the V. When you're through knitting, join the shoulder with a three-needle bind-off. Add a tiny neckband to the back and it's ready to wear.

NOTES

✤ When setting up the rib for this vest, it is important to begin with a purl stitch.

✤ To eliminate bulk from woven-in ends, splice the yarn when joining a new ball.

FINISHED SIZE
About 32 (36, 39¼, 42½, 48)" (81.5 [91.5, 99.5, 108, 122] cm) bust circumference. Vest shown measures 36" (91.5 cm).

YARN
Bulky (#6 Super Bulky).

Shown here: Dale of Norway Hubro (100% wool; 36 yd [33 m]/50 g): #5762 steel gray, 7 (8, 9, 10, 11) balls.

NEEDLES
Body—size U.S. 13 (9 mm): 24" (60 cm) circular (cir) and set of 3 double-pointed (dpn) for three-needle bind-off. Edging—size U.S. 11 (8 mm): 16" (40 cm) and 24" (60 cm) cir. Adjust needle size if necessary to obtain the correct gauge.

NOTIONS
Markers (m); stitch holders; cable needle (cn); tapestry needle.

GAUGE
10 stitches and 13 rounds = 4" (10 cm) in stockinette stitch on larger needle.

BODY

With smaller 24" (60 cm) cir needle, CO 76 (86, 94, 102, 116) sts. Place marker (pm) and join for working in rnds, being careful not to twist sts. Work even in p1, k1 rib until piece measures 4" (10 cm) from CO. Change to larger cir needle. *Inc rnd:* [K3 (4, 5, 5, 7), M1 (see Glossary)] 2 times, k4 (4, 4, 6, 6), p1, M1, k3, M1, k2, [p1, k1] 3 times, p1, k3, M1, k2, p1, M1, k4 (4, 4, 6, 6), [M1, k3 (4, 5, 5, 7)] 2 times, pm for right underarm, k5 (5, 6, 8, 8), M1, [k9 (11, 12, 12, 14), M1] 3 times, k5 (5, 5, 7, 7)—88 (98, 106, 114, 128) sts total; 47 (51, 55, 59, 67) sts for front and 41 (47, 51, 55, 61) sts for back. *Set-up rnd:* K12 (14, 16, 18, 22), work next 23 sts according to Row 1 of Cable chart, knit to end. Cont in patt as established until piece measures 9 (9, 9¾, 10, 11)" (23 [23, 25, 25.5, 28] cm) from CO, ending with an odd-number rnd of chart.

Chunky yarn makes for quick knitting.

Shape Front Neck

Note: Armhole shaping is introduced at the same time as the neck shaping is worked; read all the way through the foll sections before proceeding. Keeping in patt as established, work 23 (25, 27, 29, 33) sts, BO next st, work to end—87 (97, 105, 113, 127) sts rem. Cut yarn and slip left front sts from left needle to right needle. Rejoin yarn and work back and forth in rows, beg and ending at front neck. Work 1 WS row even. *Dec row:* Keeping in patt, work 11 sts, k2tog, work to last 13 sts, ssk (see Glossary), work to end—2 sts dec'd. Dec 1 st each side of neck in this manner every RS row 1 (1, 1, 2, 3) more times, then every 4th row 4 (4, 4, 4, 5) times. *At the same time* when piece measures 10¼ (10½, 11, 11½, 12¼)" (26 [26.5, 28, 29, 31] cm) from CO, divide for front and back.

Divide for Front and Back

Divide sts for front and back at markers, working each half separately as foll and working the 2 sts at each armhole edge in k1, p1 rib so that each selvedge st is a knit st.

Cable

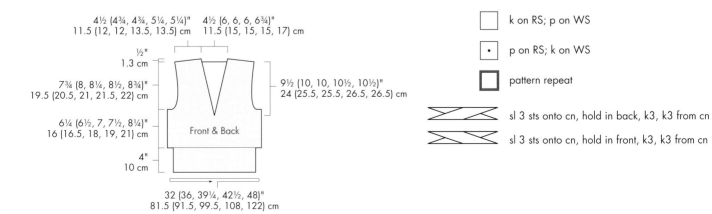

FRONT

Working each front separately back and forth in rows, dec 1 st 2 sts in from each armhole edge every 4th row 3 (4, 5, 5, 6) times—14 (15, 16, 17, 18) sts rem each side after neck and armhole shaping is complete. Cont even in patt until armholes measure 7¾ (8, 8¼, 8½, 8¾)" (19.5 [20.5, 21, 21.5, 22] cm).

Shape Shoulders

Keeping in patt as established and beg at neck edge, work short-rows (see Glossary) as foll: Work 7 (8, 8, 9, 9) sts, wrap next st, turn work, and work back to neck edge. Place all sts on holder.

BACK

Working 41 (47, 51, 55, 61) back sts back and forth in rows, dec 1 st each end of needle 2 sts in from the armhole edge every RS row 0 (0, 0, 1, 5) time(s), then every 4th row 4 (4, 6, 6, 4) times—33 (39, 39, 41, 43) sts rem. Cont even until armholes measure 7¾ (8, 8¼, 8½, 8¾)" (19.5 [20.5, 21, 21.5, 22] cm), ending with a WS row.

Shape Shoulders and Neck

Work short-rows as foll: K12 (14, 14, 15, 15), knit next 9 (11, 11, 11, 13) sts and place onto holder for neck, k6 (7, 7, 8, 8), wrap next st, turn work, purl to neck edge. Place the first 1 (2, 2, 2, 2) st(s) onto the holder with the neck sts; place rem 11 (12, 12, 13, 13) sts onto another holder for shoulder. With WS facing, join yarn to right shoulder. P6 (7, 7, 8, 8), wrap next st, turn work, knit to neck edge. Place the first 1 (2, 2, 2, 2) st(s) onto the holder with the neck sts; place rem 11 (12, 12, 13, 13) sts onto another holder for shoulder.

FINISHING

Turn work inside out. Place the right front shoulder sts on one dpn and the right back shoulder sts on another dpn. With RS facing tog, use the three-needle method (see Glossary) to BO the sts tog and *at the same time* work k2tog 3 (3, 4, 4, 5) times evenly spaced across cable panel on front. Rep for left shoulder.

Back Neckband

With smaller 16" (40 cm) cir needle, RS facing, and beg at right shoulder, pick up and knit 2 sts along back neck slope, k11 (15, 15, 15, 17) from holder, pick up and knit 2 sts along other back neck slope—15 (19, 19, 19, 21) sts total. With WS facing, BO all sts kwise.
Weave in loose ends that were not spliced. Block to measurements.

Work the front and back armhole edges in narrow ribs and skip the edgings.

design NOTEBOOK

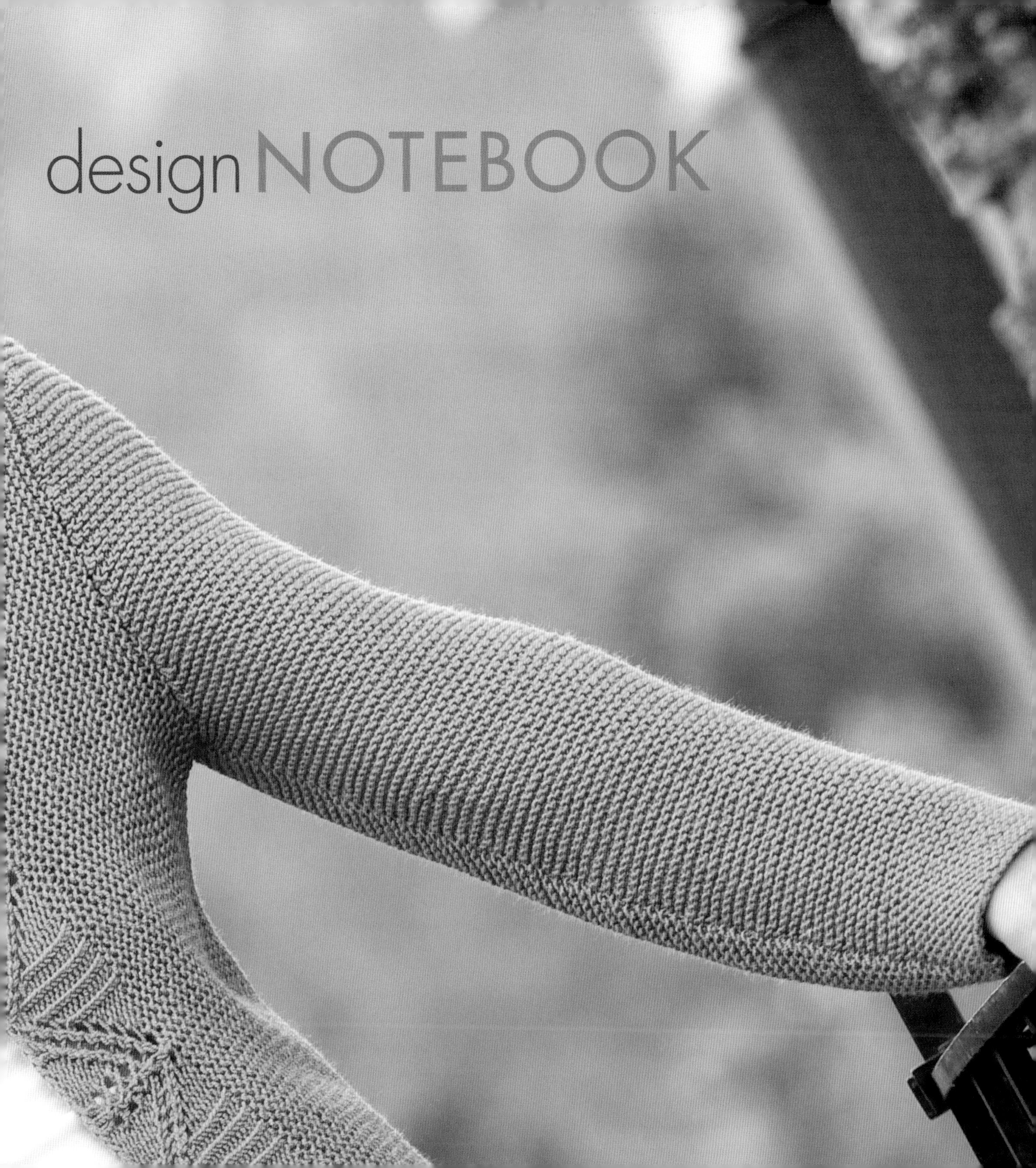

FOUR-QUARTERS PULLOVER
Pam Allen

KAZUMI PULLOVER
JoLene Treace

SIMPLIFY YOUR KNITTING

Consider the little black dress—the epitome of style and simplicity. That's what we're after in *Simple Style*. But simple doesn't mean remedial; in a simple sweater, a few design elements— executed perfectly—can result in a clean and beautiful garment. Choose a flattering silhouette, add a nonfussy detail or two, finish it expertly, and you've got a classic.

The designers who knitted garments for this book took a close look at their knitting and chose just the right mix of yarn, stitches, and silhouette to come up with designs that are beautiful and easy to knit. For starters, they limited the number of design elements and capitalized on the inherent beauty of the yarn and knitted stitches. They added just a bit of texture or color for visual interest. Following the Bohus design theory that form follows function, most of the designers found clever ways to incorporate design elements into the necessary shaping of their garments. Waists are pulled in with ribs or cables, yokes are shaped with decorative combinations of increases and decreases, and bodies flare with a change to larger needles. To keep things truly simple, many designers found ways to eliminate unnecessary details, minimize seams, and reduce finishing steps.

Focus on a few elements
for quiet beauty.

LIMIT THE NUMBER OF DESIGN ELEMENTS

You'll find that most of the garments in this book feature just one or two elements of design. Rather than making the garments look ordinary or boring, these elements stand out in quiet elegance. In her Four-Quarters Pullover (page 12), Pam Allen chose a hand-dyed yarn with relatively bold color striations for a classic flared shape that she knitted in four easy pieces. She seamed the pieces along the tops of the sleeves, sides, and center front and back, but she turned the selvedges of the center front and back seams to the public side to accentuate the breaks in the color striations. JoLene Treace used a decorative cast-on and added just a scattering of eyelets along the hem and cuffs of her otherwise simply ribbed Kazumi Pullover (page 30). The hem of Kat Coyle's Short-Row Skirt (page 44) is gracefully punctuated with vertical columns of eyelets. Vicki Square made the neckband the focus of her Kimono Classic (page 58) by leaving the lower end free to tuck into a tab closure. All of these garments are striking in their simplicity.

SIMPLIFY STITCH AND COLOR PATTERNS

The first step to simple knitting is choosing a stitch pattern that's easy to work and memorize. Most of the designs in this book are based on stitch patterns that have short repeats, in terms of both stitches and rows. By far the simplest of these is garter stitch—simply knit every stitch of every row. Other than the lace bands that decorate the front opening, Ann Budd worked her Garter Lace Jacket (page 98) entirely in garter stitch. Most of the designs, such as Margaret Hubert's Kokopelli Jacket (page 36), are worked in stockinette stitch, which involves the soothing repetition of alternating a right-side row of knit stitches with a wrong-side row of purl stitches. For those stockinette-stitch projects that are worked in rounds, such as Katie Himmelberg's Kaleidoscope Yoke (page 40), every "row" is a right-side row and only knit stitches are required.

For projects that involved more complicated stitch patterns, the designers chose to limit amount and placement. Take Kat Coyle's Guernsey Skirt (page 76), for example. Although Kat incorporated several texture patterns in her skirt—ladder stitch, cables, moss stitch, and ribs—none of these repeats over more than eight stitches or eight rows. And because all of the patterns repeat evenly in the eight rows of the cable, by keeping track of the cable rows, she could keep track of all the other patterns.

Celebrate the knit stitch.

SHORT-ROW SKIRT
Kat Coyle

GARTER LACE JACKET
Ann Budd

STAY-PUT WRAP
Mags Kandis

ORGANIC COTTON HENLEY
Micki Hair

For simplicity, most designers limited the fancy stitches to areas that were free of any shaping increases or decreases. Kat included hip shaping in her skirt, but she cleverly confined it to the knit-one-purl-one ribs at the sides, where it didn't interfere with the larger stitch patterns. Mags Kandis placed a twenty-stitch braided cable along the side of her Stay-Put Wrap (page 94), but she positioned it well out of the way of the bind-off and cast-on stitches for the armhole slits. Deborah Newton incorporated a couple of seemingly complicated cable and lace patterns in her Drawstring Bateau (page 48), but because the bateau has no armhole or neck shaping, no increases or decreases impede the stitch patterns. This consideration is especially important in lace patterns where shaping can interrupt the increase/decrease combinations of the lace and throw off the pattern integrity.

Probably the most complicated stitch pattern in this book is the lace edge on Ann Budd's Garter Lace Jacket (page 98). The lace follows a relatively complex eighteen-stitch pattern that involves twisted stitches on both right- and wrong-side rows. However, Ann limited the pattern to the straight edges of the center fronts, before the neck shaping was introduced.

In her Weekend Fair Isle (page 90), Ann E. Smith combined texture and color patterns but used a boxy shape so that the shaping wouldn't interfere with the patterns. To keep the knitting simple, she chose color patterns that involved only two colors per row, and that repeated over an easily memorized six stitches. Micki Hair added a refreshing touch of color to the edges of her Organic Cotton Henley (page 24) by simply working three rows of knit-one-purl-one ribbing in a contrasting color, then enhancing it with flower motifs embroidered in place after the knitting was complete.

A little bit of pattern goes a long way.

ELIMINATE SEAMS

Not many knitters relish seaming the pieces of a garment together, and many hurry through the process to get it over with as soon as possible. Yet a single poorly sewn seam can ruin an otherwise beautiful sweater. With this in mind, many of the designers included in this book found ways to eliminate seams from their garments.

The best way to eliminate seams is to work a garment in the round. A pullover can be worked entirely in the round, either from the bottom up or from the top down. Katie Himmelberg cast on stitches for the neck of her Kaleidoscope Yoke (page 40), worked in rounds while increasing to the base of armholes, then separated the body and sleeves and worked each separately (also in rounds) to the lower edge. She also avoided seams in her Best-Fit Jumper (page 86) by casting on stitches for the top of the bodice and working in rounds to the hem. By picking up stitches along the top of the bodice for the shoulder straps, she managed to avoid even those short seams. Skirts are also easy to work in rounds because you needn't deal with armholes. Kat Coyle simply knitted a tapered tube for her Guernsey Skirt (page 76). She cast on stitches for the full circumference at the hem, then worked decreases to the narrower circumference at the waist.

The front opening of a cardigan negates working in rounds, but you can still eliminate the side seams by working the fronts and back in a single piece. Take Cecily Glowik's Sixteen-Button Cardigan (page 18), for example. Cecily worked the body back and forth in rows from the hem to the underarms, set the body aside while she worked the sleeves in rounds from the cuffs to the underarms, then joined the pieces and worked the yoke in a single piece to the neck. Véronik Avery took a similar approach with her Offset Raglan (page 80), but instead of placing the front opening at the center, she moved it off center for an unexpected and stylish asymmetry. Therese Chynoweth also eliminated side and sleeve seams in her Empire Swing Cardigan (page 70) by working the fronts and back together and the sleeves in rounds to the armholes.

Another way to forego seams is to use the three-needle bind-off technique (see Glossary) to join live stitches. This technique is especially useful for joining shoulder seams. Vicki Square used it for her Kimono Classic (page 58), and Therese Chynoweth used it for her Big Cable Vest (page 102).

For many knitters, armhole seams are the most difficult to sew. However, it's possible to eliminate these seams by picking up stitches around the armholes and working the sleeves down. It's easiest if the garment has drop-shoulder shaping, as do Micki Hair's Organic Cotton Henley (page 24) and Mags Kandis's Stay-Put Wrap (page 94). Both designers continued the seamless approach by working the sleeves in the round to the cuffs.

BEST-FIT JUMPER
Katie Himmelberg

EMPIRE SWING CARDIGAN
Therese Chynoweth

BIG CABLE VEST
Therese Chynoweth

FOUR-QUARTERS PULLOVER
Pam Allen

MINIMIZE EDGINGS

You can streamline the finishing process if you minimize the number of edgings that are sewn on or picked up and knitted onto a garment. Although edgings can add visual interest as they tidy up raw edges, they aren't always necessary, especially if you use noncurling stitch patterns such as ribbing or garter stitch. In many cases, cast-on, bind-off, and selvedge edges are fine by themselves.

JoLene Treace used a decorative Channel Island cast-on to produce a delicate "string of pearls" along the hem and cuffs of her Kazumi Pullover (page 30). She then worked the pullover in a noncurling rib pattern that she extended into the neckband. The lace pattern that Ann Budd placed along the front edges of her Garter Lace Jacket (page 98) produces a slightly scalloped edge that makes an attractive contrast to the linear garter ridges in the rest of the jacket. The ribs within the lace pattern prevent it from curling.

Both Katie Himmelberg's Kaleidoscope Yoke (page 40) and Margaret Hubert's Kokopelli Jacket (page 36) were worked entirely in stockinette stitch. But rather than add edgings to prevent the cast-on and bind-off edges from curling, they let the natural roll become a design element. Micki Hair also incorporated rolled edges in her Organic Cotton Henley (page 24), but she controlled the extent of the roll by working a few rows of single rib after an inch of stockinette stitch.

It's also possible to work a stabilizing edging at the same time that you work the body of a garment. For example, Therese Chynoweth worked a few stitches in single rib at each armhole and neck edge of her Big Cable Vest (page 102). The ribs pulled in to form tidy edges without any extra work. Pam Allen stabilized the selvedges along the cuffs of her Four-Quarters Pullover (page 12) by working a couple of edge stitches in garter stitch (knitted every row). She also left the selvedges exposed in the inside-out center seams on the front and back. To keep these selvedges tidy, Pam worked the edge stitches in garter stitch as well.

Don't mess with a
good thing.

REDUCE BUTTONHOLES

Buttonholes can require a lot of planning. Because you work them as you knit the piece, you need to know the exact length of the opening needed to accommodate the size of the buttons before you begin. You must then work the buttonholes at even intervals as you knit, which involves stopping to count stitches and rows along the way. To simplify your next cardigan, consider one of the following alternatives, which you'll find in the *Simple Style* projects.

Margaret Hubert fastened her Kokopelli Jacket (page 36) with a single button at the neck. She made a large buttonhole and found an oversize button to fit. She didn't have to plan for spacing several buttons or worry about the size of the buttonhole. And it looks great! Instead of buttons, Véronik Avery fastened her Offset Raglan (page 80) with large hook-and-eye closures that she sewed in place after the front bands were knitted. The no-see closure gives a sleek, trim look to her jacket. For another alternative, Vicki Square knitted a short tab through which she tucked the free end of the left neckband for a crossover closure in her Kimono Classic (page 58). And don't forget that some garments look and fit fine without any type of closure at all. Take Ann Budd's Garter Lace Jacket (page 98), for instance. The decorative lace bands along the fronts hang open from the neck to the hem.

MAKE THE MOST OF WHAT YOU'VE GOT

Garment shaping doesn't have to rely on a series of planned increases or decreases. Think about how needle size and stitch patterns can affect the shape of a garment and you'll find all sorts of ways to introduce fit and style as you knit.

Needle Up and Needle Down

One of the easiest ways to add shape to a garment is to adjust the size of needles as you knit—larger needles will result in larger stitches and consequently, larger dimensions; smaller needles will result in smaller stitches and smaller dimensions. To create the flare at the hem of her Four-Quarters Pullover (page 12), Pam Allen cast on with larger needles, then changed to progressively smaller needles as she approached the waist, ending up with the needle size that gave her the desired stitch gauge. Margaret Hubert gave shape to the collar on her Kokopelli Jacket (page 36) by changing to larger needles at the point where she wanted the collar to fold over. To prevent the ribbed pattern from drawing in the stitches of the "skirt" of her Empire Swing Cardigan (page 70), Therese Chynoweth worked that section on larger needles than she used for the bodice or sleeves.

Add flare without
increases or decreases.

OFFSET RAGLAN
Véronik Avery

KOKOPELLI JACKET
Margaret Hubert

LET THE STITCHES WORK FOR YOU

Rather than stress over how and where to work increases and decreases to get the shape you want, choose stitch patterns that will do the work for you. Many designers rely on the elasticity of ribbing to shape parts of their garments. For example, Katie Himmelberg worked the bodice of her Best-Fit Jumper (page 86) in a knit-three-purl-two rib so that it would stretch for a custom fit. For a similar personalized fit, Ruthie Nussbaum added single (knit-one-purl-one) ribs along each side of her Tailored Vest (page 64). Alice Halbeisen also used single ribs to shape the waist of her Twisted-V Pullover (page 52), but she extended the ribs to the base of the neckline for a body-hugging look. Kat Coyle worked single ribs in conjunction with decreases along the sides to taper her Guernsey Skirt (page 76) from the hips to the waist. For her Short-Row Skirt (page 44), Kat worked from side to side while incorporating short-rows to produce the gentle flare at the bottom (resulting in more rows around the hem than around the waist).

Cables are notorious for causing fabric draw-in, so much so that designers often add extra stitches to counteract this tendency. However, Deborah Newton used cable draw-in to her advantage to help shape the waist of her Drawstring Bateau (page 48). In addition, she cleverly worked eyelets into the pattern to accommodate a drawstring for added shaping.

Get your stretch from ribbing.

TAILORED VEST
Ruthie Nussbaum

GUERNSEY SKIRT
Kat Coyle

DRAWSTRING BATEAU
Deborah Newton

PUT AN END TO ENDS

Weaving in loose ends of yarn can take a lot of unnecessary time when you're anxious to start wearing your garment. To minimize the chore, try these time-saving techniques.

Splice Yarns

If you work with a yarn that's predominantly wool (excluding superwash varieties), you can eliminate weaving in yarn tails by splicing yarns together when you join a new ball. Simply untwist a couple of inches of plies from the end of each ball (Figure 1), overlap the raveled ends (Figure 2), moisten them with water (or saliva), and rub them vigorously between the palms of your hands (Figure 3). The moisture and friction will cause the two yarn ends to felt together.

Figure 1

Figure 2

Figure 3

Weave in Ends as You Knit

Another way to avoid weaving in so many tails at the end of a project is to weave in tails as you knit. With the right side of the work facing you, catch the tail over and under the working yarn for several stitches to hold it in place. After a few rows of knitting, trim the tail, leaving about ½" (1.3 cm) hanging on the wrong side to prevent the tail from working its way to the right side of the piece. How you weave in the ends depends on whether you use the English or Continental method of knitting.

English Method: Hold the tail of the old yarn over your left index finger and the new working yarn over your right index finger. *Insert the needle into the stitch, then under the old yarn. Wrap the new yarn around the needle as usual, bring the needle out from under the old yarn and through the stitch, then knit the following stitch as usual. Repeat from * two or three times to secure the old yarn.

Continental Method: Hold the tail of the old yarn (light) over your left index finger and the new working yarn (dark) over both your index and middle fingers so that it's to the right of the old yarn. *Insert the needle into the stitch and under the old yarn (Figure 1) and knit the stitch with the new yarn. Then insert the needle into the following stitch and over the old yarn (Figure 2) and knit the next stitch with the new yarn. Repeat from * two or three times to secure the old yarn.

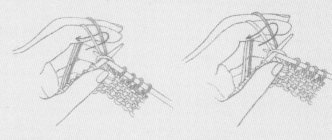

Figure 1   Figure 2

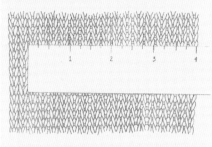

Figure 1

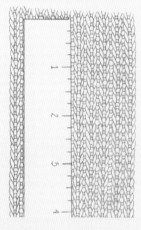

Figure 2

ESSENTIAL TECHNIQUES

Simple projects require close attention to the details, maybe even more than complicated projects, in which many design elements make individual techniques less noticeable. However, if you follow a few essential guidelines, you're sure to enjoy success along the way.

Stay on Gauge

The first step of any project is knitting a gauge swatch to make sure that you get the same gauge (number of stitches and rows per inch of knitting) as specified in the instructions. Although knitting needles come in standard sizes, the sizes can vary between manufacturers. A size 5 (3.75 mm) needle from one company may more closely resemble a size 4 (3.5 mm) or size 6 (4 mm) needle from another. In addition, needles are manufactured from all sorts of materials—steel, aluminum, bamboo, exotic woods, and resin, to name a few. Interestingly, the material of the needles can affect the ease with which different yarns are manipulated into stitches, which in turn can affect the size of the stitches. Therefore, it's important to knit your gauge swatch with the exact needles and yarn you plan to use for your project.

If you plan to knit your garment in the round, knit the gauge swatch in the round. Many knitters knit a little more tightly than they purl or vice versa. If this is true for you, your gauge will be slightly different when you work stockinette stitch in rounds, when the right side is always facing you and every stitch is a knit stitch, than it is when you work back and forth, alternating rows of knit stitches with rows of purl stitches. For some knitters, the difference in tension between knit and purl rows is so dramatic that they use different size needles for knit and purl rows.

To begin, knit a swatch at least 6" (15 cm) square in the specified stitch pattern. (The bigger the swatch, the better it will represent how the stitches will behave in the finished garment.) Bind off the stitches loosely, then wash the swatch the same way you plan to wash the finished garment. When the swatch is dry, place it on a flat surface to measure gauge. Place a ruler (not a tape measure, which can stretch and give inaccurate measurements) over the swatch and count the number of stitches across (Figure 1) and the number of rows down (Figure 2), including fractions of stitches and rows, in a 4" (10 cm) segment. Divide this number by four to get the number of stitches (including fractions of stitches) in one inch. Repeat two or three times on different areas of the swatch to confirm your measurements. If you have more stitches and rows than called for in the instructions, knit another swatch with larger needles; if you have fewer stitches and rows, knit another swatch with smaller needles.

MEASURE AS YOU KNIT

Because the fabric is shaped as it is knitted, it's important to take accurate measurements as you go. Unlike sewn garments, most handknits are not constructed out of pieces that have been cut and shaped from a flat piece of cloth. Instead, the shape of a piece is created as the fabric is created. Therefore, it's essential to measure the pieces accurately along the way to ensure that the shaping is worked on the appropriate rows.

To measure a piece in progress, lay it on a hard flat surface, such as the floor or the top of a table. Smooth out the stitches so that they aren't bunched together on the needles. You may want to measure when you're halfway through a row, when the stitches are divided between two needles, or temporarily place the stitches on a string. Smooth out the fabric along the length and width, pulling it slightly widthwise to mimic the effects of blocking. Uncurl the edges to expose the selvedges. Place a yardstick across the piece horizontally, well away from the influence of the cast-on edge, any edge-stitch pattern, or the needles. The edge of the yardstick should be even with one selvedge edge to measure the width to the other selvedge edge (Figure 1). With the piece still smoothed out, place the yardstick along the piece vertically, with the end of the stick even with the base of the knitting needles to measure the length to the cast-on edge (Figure 2).

Measure the widthwise dimensions periodically to make sure that the piece is indeed the anticipated size. Don't be surprised if you discover that your gauge changed slightly after you had the full number of stitches on the needles and got into the groove of knitting. As a result of the change, the piece may be larger or smaller than you intended (this happens even to expert knitters). The solution is to rip out and start again with a different needle size or a different number of stitches. If this happens to you, be glad that you found the discrepancy early on when there was less to rip out.

TAILORED VEST
Ruthie Nussbaum

Plan ahead to eliminate work later.

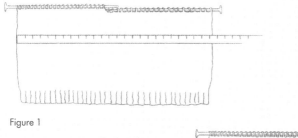

Figure 1

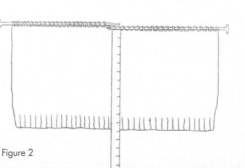

Figure 2

DRAWSTRING BATEAU
Deborah Newton

KAZUMI PULLOVER
JoLene Treace

SEAM DETAILS

If your garment is constructed with seams, you can ensure a professional look by taking time to make sure the seams are neat and tidy. The precursors to beautiful seams are properly prepared edges.

Selvedge Stitches

For many of us, the very first stitch and the very last stitch of each row are somewhat mis-shapen, especially if these edge stitches are involved in increases or decreases. The result can be seams that pull or pucker. You can help minimize these variations by working the edge stitches in garter stitch (knit them every row), regardless of what stitch pattern is used for the rest of the garment—the selvedge stitches will be hidden in the seam. Keep the integrity of the selvedge stitches by working all shaping increases and decreases at least one stitch from the edge. When working a decrease row at the armhole, for example, knit the selvedge stitch, work the decrease of your choice, then work across the row to the other end, work another decrease, then knit the remaining selvedge stitch.

Count Rows for Length

No matter how well you sew your seams, they will pucker if the pieces to be seamed are not the same length. Because knitted fabric stretches in both width and length, it's easy to convince yourself that two pieces are the same length when, in fact, they're not. The only way to ensure that they are the same is to count the number of rows in each. It's quite easy to count rows when the purl side of stockinette stitch is facing you. Each horizontal ridge (consisting of a convex and a concave crescent) represents a single row of knitting. Hold the edge of the knitting in your hands and pull gently to separate the ridges. Then use a knitting needle or your thumb to count off the horizontal ridges. You might find it helpful to place removable markers in every tenth ridge as you go, then count the markers.

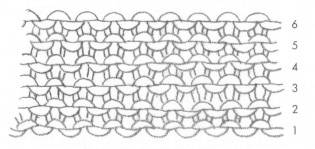

Each horizontal ridge represents one row.

Block the Pieces Before Seaming

Block the pieces to be seamed to even out the stitches and reduce curling. Consider investing in a set of blocking wires for this purpose. Slip the wires through the edge stitches of the damp pieces (this is most easily done if the edge stitches are worked in garter stitch), then pull on the wires until the desired dimensions are achieved. Use rustproof T-pins to pin the wires in place on a padded surface (such as a bed or carpet) and allow the pieces to air-dry before removing the wires. If you don't have blocking wires, lay the pieces flat on the padded surface and use pins to straighten the selvedge edges. (For more information about blocking, see page 123).

Beautiful seams depend on properly prepared edges.

EMPIRE SWING CARDIGAN

Therese Chynoweth

ORGANIC COTTON HENLEY

Micki Hair

PAIRED INCREASES

In this book, the designers used two common types of increases—raised increases and lifted increases—to produce a stitch that slants subtly to the right or left.

Raised Increase

Also called "make one (M1)," a raised increase is worked into the horizontal strand that lies between two stitches. The horizontal strand is lifted onto the left needle, then knitted in such a way as to twist the stitch and thereby prevent a hole. This type of increase is often specified for colorwork or other patterns in which it's important that the increase not affect the stitches already on the needles.

Left Slant (M1L)

Note: If no direction of slant is specified in the instructions, use the left slant.

With the left needle tip, lift the strand between the last knitted stitch and the first stitch on the left needle from front to back (Figure 1), then knit the lifted loop through the back (Figure 2).

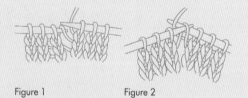

Figure 1   Figure 2

Right Slant (M1R)

With the left needle tip, lift the strand between the needles from back to front (Figure 1). Knit the lifted loop through the front (Figure 2).

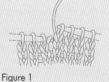

Figure 1   Figure 2

Lifted Increase

The lifted increase is performed by working into the stitch in the row below the stitch that's on the needle, then working the stitch on the needle as usual. It's ideal for increasing stitches in the middle of a piece where you want the increase to be fairly inconspicuous. If the increases are to be stacked one on top of another in the same location, as for the front of a skirt worked from waist to hem, space the lifted increases at least three rows apart to prevent them from pulling up the work and distorting the overall appearance.

Left Slant (LLI)

Note: If no slant direction is specified in the instructions, use the right slant.

Knit into the back of the stitch (in the "purl bump") in the row directly below the stitch on the needle (Figure 1), then knit the stitch on the needle (Figure 2), and slip the original stitch off the needle.

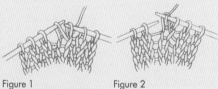

Figure 1   Figure 2

Right Slant (RLI)

Insert the left needle tip into the back of the stitch below the stitch just knitted (Figure 1), then knit this stitch (Figure 2).

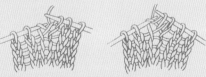

Figure 1   Figure 2

PAIRED DECREASES

Paired decreases are often used to shape the armholes and necks of garments worked from the bottom up. Designers often choose to work left-slanting decreases at the right edge (at the beginning of right-side rows) and right-slanting decreases on the left edge (at the end of right-side rows). If they work the decreases a few stitches in from the edges, the decrease line becomes pronounced and the resulting shaping is called "full-fashioned." If you prefer to minimize the appearance of the decreases, work them in the opposite order—right-slanting decreases at the right edge and left-slanting decreases at the left edge.

Left-Slant Decreases

Viewed from a right-side row, the top stitch of a left-slanting decrease leans toward the left.

Slip, Slip, Knit (ssk)

Slip two stitches individually knitwise (Figure 1), insert left needle tip into the front of these two slipped stitches, and use the right needle to knit them together through their back loops (Figure 2).

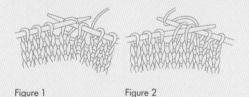

Figure 1   Figure 2

Slip, Slip, Purl (ssp)

Holding the yarn in front, slip two stitches individually knitwise (Figure 1), then slip these two stitches back onto the left needle (they will be turned on the needle) and purl them together through their back loops (Figure 2).

Figure 1   Figure 2

Right-Slant Decreases

Viewed from a right-side row, the top stitch of a right-slanting decrease leans toward the right.

Knit 2 Together (k2tog)

Knit two stitches together as if they were a single stitch.

Purl 2 Together (p2tog)

Purl two stitches together as if they were a single stitch.

TWISTED-V PULLOVER
Alice Halbeisen

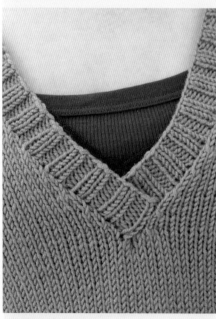

TAILORED VEST
Ruthie Nussbaum

PAIRED INCREASES AND DECREASES

Many designs, even simple ones, rely on increases and decreases to produce the desired shapes. There are a handful of ways to add or subtract stitches, and savvy designers know that the type of increase or decrease they choose can have a big impact on the overall look of their garments. Depending on how they're worked, increases can slant to the left or right. Many of us learned to decrease a stitch by just knitting two stitches together, and we used this right-slanting method whenever a decrease was in order—at the right edge, at the left edge, or within the center of a row of knitting. What a revelation it was to learn that the stitches could be mirrored to enhance the shaping or produce a symmetrical look!

For an example of the different looks, consider Alice Halbeisen's Twisted-V Pullover (page 52) and Ruthie Nussbaum's Tailored Vest (page 64). Both designers shaped their armholes and V-necks with left- and right-leaning decreases. Alice chose to work left-leaning decreases along the left-slanting edges and right-leaning decreases along the right-slanting edges to emphasize the shaping lines along the armholes and neck of her pullover. Ruthie did the reverse to de-emphasize the same lines on her vest. Both are good design options. In her Kokopelli Jacket (page 36), Margaret Hubert followed Alice's lead in working armhole decreases that slant in the same direction as the shaping, but she placed the decreases a couple of stitches in from the edges for an even more pronounced line.

Katie Himmelberg paired left- and right-leaning raised (make-one) increases and aligned the pairs to form four wide "gores" in the skirt of her Best-Fit Jumper (page 86). She used the same type of increases to shape the yoke of her Kaleidoscope Yoke pullover (page 40) in eight sections, capitalizing on the way the increases made angles in the stripe sequence to produce the kaleidoscopic look.

For her Offset Raglan (page 80), Véronik Avery paired left- and right-leaning double decreases with a few purl stitches in between to form decorative patterns along the four raglan lines. Although any type of decrease would suffice to shape the raglans, the cablelike look of Véronik's combination adds an elegant focus to the design.

Not all decreases and increases are created equal.

BLOCKING

Blocking is essential to give a knitted garment a polished and finished look. Adding moisture makes the fabric easier to manipulate, letting you impart to the garment the desired permanent size and shape. As fabric is blocked, the individual stitches are smoothed out to take a more uniform look, and the texture and drape are set in the fabric. For lace and openwork patterns, blocking is essential to bring out the texture and drape. You can add moisture several ways and to different degrees depending on the kind of fabric and what you need to have the blocking accomplish. *Note:* Always block away from direct sun or heat.

Steam-Blocking

Steam-blocking is most effective on wool and wool-blend yarns that can be stretched and shaped with just a small amount of moisture. For best results, use an iron set on the lowest possible steam setting. Pin the knitted piece wrong side up on a padded surface. You can use your ironing board for small pieces and a table top padded with a few layers of bath towels for larger pieces. Hold the iron at least ½" (1.3 cm) above the surface of the knitting, allowing the steam to penetrate the fibers without touching the iron to the yarn. Work from the top to the bottom of the piece (not side to side, which can distort the stitches) and allow the fabric to cool and dry before removing the pins.

> Blocking smoothes out the individual stitches.

KIMONO CLASSIC

Vicki Square

KALEIDOSCOPE YOKE

Katie Himmelberg

OFFSET RAGLAN

Véronik Avery

WEEKEND FAIR ISLE
Ann E. Smith

SIXTEEN-BUTTON CARDIGAN
Cecily Glowik

Wet-Blocking

Wet-blocking uses more moisture than steam-blocking. Three "degrees" of wet-blocking add different amounts of moisture.

Spray-blocking, the mildest form of wet-blocking, works for all types of fibers. You'll find that silks and synthetics require more moisture than wool. On a padded surface, pin the knitted piece right side up to the desired shape. Fill a spray bottle with lukewarm tap water and spritz a fine, even mist over the entire surface. Use your hands to gently pat the moisture into the knitted fabric, but be careful not to flatten any textured stitches such as cables or ribs. Let the piece dry thoroughly before removing the pins.

Wet-wrapping imparts moisture deeper into the fibers. It works well on all types of fibers but is recommended for cotton and acrylic, which require more moisture to reshape the stitches. To begin, thoroughly soak a large bath towel in water, then run it through the spin cycle of your washing machine to remove excess moisture. Arrange the knitted piece in a single layer on top of the towel, then roll it up jelly-roll fashion. Let the bundle sit until the yarn is completely damp (overnight if necessary). Unroll the towel, remove the knitted piece, and pin it out to the desired shape on a padded surface. Let it dry thoroughly before removing the pins.

Immersion is the most extreme form of blocking. Although it's appropriate for all fiber types, it's particularly useful for heavily textured fabrics or fabrics that have taken on a biased slant during knitting. It's also the method to use after you wash a handknit. Soak the knitted piece in a basin of lukewarm water for about twenty minutes or until the core of the yarn is wet. Gently squeeze water through the piece if necessary. Drain the water from the basin and squeeze excess water out of the fabric, being careful not to twist or wring the stitches. Carry the piece in a bundle to the washing machine and run it through the spin cycle (or roll it in dry towels) to remove additional moisture. Shape and pin the piece to the desired shape on a padded surface. Let it dry thoroughly before removing the pins.

THE ABCs OF SIMPLE KNITTING

Ask for help if you run into problems. Knitting shops are full of kind, helpful people who have a vested interest in your success.

Block the pieces before seaming a garment to facilitate sewing.

Count rows to make sure the pieces are the same length to the armholes. Count stitches periodically to make sure you haven't inadvertently added or lost a stitch during a row.

Decrease with stitches that slant to the left or right to enhance your shaping lines.

Exercise your arms, hands, and fingers by stretching them periodically to prevent cramps and avoid aggravating repetitive-motion symptoms.

Finish a row before putting down your knitting. Stopping in the center of a row can cause uneven stitches and risk dropped stitches.

Gauge the number of stitches and rows per inch by swatching. The success of your project depends on it.

Have fun. Remember, knitting is a hobby; it isn't a race and it isn't rocket science.

Indulge in quality yarn and needles that make knitting a pleasure.

Jot down pertinent information regarding a project so you'll have a record for future reference.

Knit when waiting at doctors' offices or sporting events. You'll be surprised how much progress you can make during these "stolen" opportunities.

Laugh at your mistakes and learn from them.

Mark separate patterns or pattern repeats with removable markers.

Notice how the stitches interact with each other on the needles and in the fabric to become familiar with the structure of knitting. It will make mistakes easier to identify.

Optimize your enjoyment by knitting in a well-lit area, especially if you're working with dark yarn.

Pair increases and decreases for a symmetrical and polished look.

Quit when you're tired or frustrated with a pattern. Chances are that it won't seem so daunting when you're fresh and rested.

Read all sections of the instructions before you proceed. Doing so will alert you to what's coming up and help you prepare for the next step.

Sew seams carefully to avoid unsightly puckers.

Take time to do your best job. Don't rush things and risk sloppy results.

Understand the techniques specified in the instructions. Refer to the glossary if you're in doubt.

Verify your gauge periodically to make sure that your garment will end up the size you intended.

Watch for knitting errors as you go. It's much less frustrating to rip out a few stitches than several inches of knitting.

eXpand your knitting know-how by trying one (and only one) new technique in each project.

You are the boss of your knitting—make each project your own!

Zero in on success by taking the process one step at a time.

ABBREVIATIONS

beg	begin(s); beginning	rem	remain(s); remaining
BO	bind off	rep	repeat(s); repeating
CC	contrasting color	rev St st	reverse stockinette stitch
cm	centimeter(s)	rnd(s)	round(s)
cn	cable needle	RS	right side
CO	cast on	sl	slip
cont	continue(s); continuing	sl st	slip st (slip 1 stitch purlwise unless otherwise indicated)
dec(s)	decrease(s); decreasing	ssk	slip 2 stitches individually knitwise from the left needle to right needle, insert left needle tip through both front loops and knit together from this position (1 stitch decrease)
dpn	double-pointed needles		
foll	follow(s); following		
g	gram(s)	st(s)	stitch(es)
inc(s)	increase(s); increasing	St st	stockinette stitch
k	knit	tbl	through back loop
k1f&b	knit into the front and back of same stitch	tog	together
kwise	knitwise, as if to knit	WS	wrong side
m	marker(s)	wyb	with yarn in back
MC	main color	wyf	with yarn in front
mm	millimeter(s)	yd	yard(s)
M1	make one (increase)	yo	yarnover
p	purl	*	repeat starting point
p1f&b	purl into front and back of same stitch	* *	repeat all instructions between asterisks
patt(s)	pattern(s)	( )	alternate measurements and/or instructions
psso	pass slipped stitch over	[ ]	work instructions as a group a specified number of times
pwise	purlwise, as if to purl		

BIND-OFFS

Standard Bind-Off

Knit the first stitch, *knit the next stitch (two stitches on right needle), insert left needle tip into first stitch on right needle (Figure 1) and lift this stitch up and over the second stitch (Figure 2) and off the needle (Figure 3). Repeat from * for the desired number of stitches.

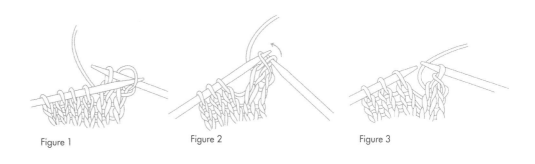

Figure 1   Figure 2   Figure 3

Three-Needle Bind-Off

Place the stitches to be joined onto two separate needles and hold the needles parallel so that the right sides of the knitting face together. Insert a third needle into the first stitch on each of the two needles (Figure 1) and knit them together as a single stitch (Figure 2). *Knit the next stitch on each needle the same way, then use the left needle tip to lift the first stitch over the second and off the needle (Figure 3). Repeat from * until no stitches remain on the first two needles. Cut the yarn and pull the tail through the last stitch to secure it.

Figure 1

Figure 2

Figure 3

BUTTONHOLES

One-Row Buttonhole

Bring the yarn to the front of the work, slip the next stitch purlwise, then return the yarn to the back. *Slip the next stitch, pass the second stitch over the slipped stitch (Figure 1) and drop it off the needle. Repeat from * two more times. Slip the last stitch on the right needle to the left needle and turn the work around. Bring the working yarn to the back, [insert the right needle between the first and second stitches on the left needle (Figure 2), draw up a loop and place it on the left needle] four times. Turn the work around. With the yarn in back, slip the first stitch and pass the extra cast-on stitch over it (Figure 3) and off the needle to complete the buttonhole.

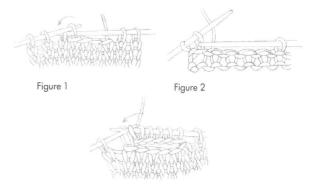

Figure 1   Figure 2

Figure 3

Simple Two-Stitch Buttonhole (yo, k2tog)

Work to where you want the buttonhole to be, yarnover, k2tog, work to end of row or to next buttonhole position. On the next row, work the yarnover in pattern as an ordinary stitch to leave a small hole and complete the buttonhole.

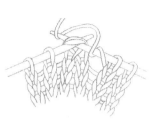

CAST-ONS

Backward-Loop Cast-On

*Loop working yarn and place it on needle backward so that it doesn't unwind. Repeat from *.

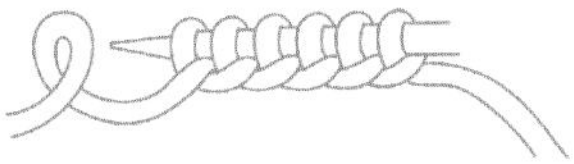

Cable Cast-On

If there are no stitches on the needles, make a slipknot of working yarn and place it on the needle, then use the knitted method to cast-on one more stitch—two stitches on needle. Hold needle with working yarn in your left hand. *Insert right needle between the first two stitches on left needle (Figure 1), wrap yarn around needle as if to knit, draw yarn through (Figure 2), and place new loop on left needle (Figure 3) to form a new stitch. Repeat from * for the desired number of stitches, always working between the first two stitches on the left needle.

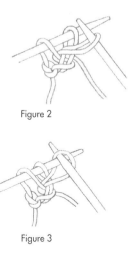

Figure 1

Figure 2

Figure 3

Channel Island Cast-On

Holding two strands of yarn together and leaving long tails (about 1" [2.5 cm] per stitch), make a slipknot on one needle. The slipknot counts as the first stitch. Cut off one strand of yarn, leaving a short tail to weave in later. Place the remaining single strand over your left index finger and wrap the double strands counterclockwise around your thumb two times. *Make a yarnover on the needle with the single strand (Figure 1). Insert needle up through both loops on your thumb, grab the single strand, and bring it back through the two thumb loops (Figure 2). Drop the thumb loops and tighten all three yarns to form two more stitches. Repeat from * for the desired number of stitches.

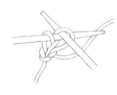

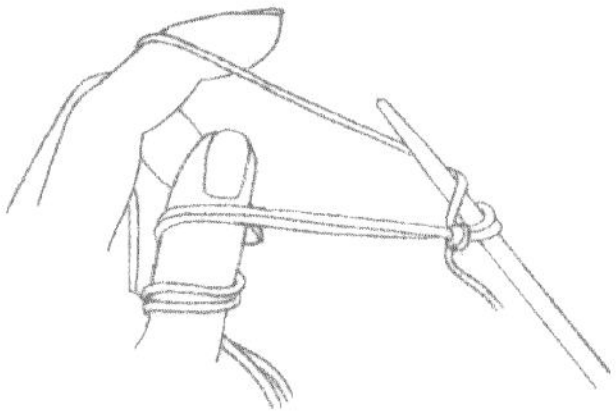

Figure 1

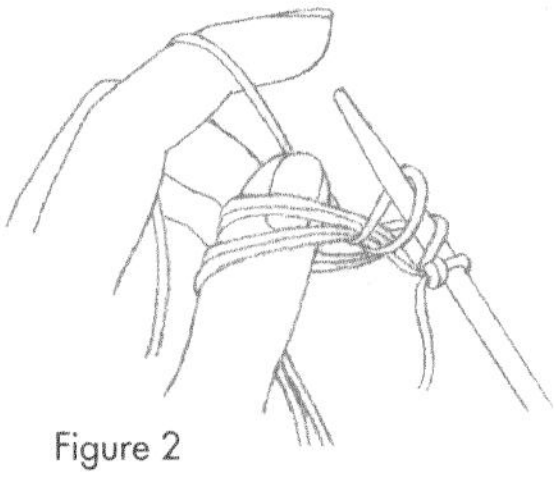

Figure 2

Knitted Cast-On

Make a slipknot of working yarn and place it on the left needle if there are no stitches already there. *Use the right needle to knit the first stitch (or slipknot) on left needle (Figure 1) and place new loop onto left needle to form a new stitch (Figure 2). Repeat from * for the desired number of stitches, always working into the last stitch made.

Figure 1

Figure 2

Long-Tail (Continental) Cast-On

Leaving a long tail (about ½" [1.3 cm] for each stitch to be cast on), make a slipknot and place on right needle. Place thumb and index finger of your left hand between the yarn ends so that working yarn is around your index finger and tail end is around your thumb and secure the yarn ends with your other fingers. Hold your palm upward, making a V of yarn (Figure 1). *Bring needle up through loop on thumb (Figure 2), catch first strand around index finger, and go back down through loop on thumb (Figure 3). Drop loop off thumb and, placing thumb back in V configuration, tighten resulting stitch on needle (Figure 4). Repeat from * for the desired number of stitches.

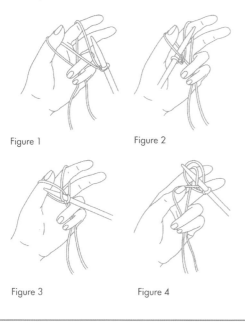

Figure 1   Figure 2

Figure 3   Figure 4

CROCHET

Crochet Chain (ch)

Make a slipknot and place it on crochet hook if there isn't a loop already on the hook. *Yarn over hook and draw through loop on hook. Repeat from * for the desired number of stitches. To fasten off, cut yarn and draw end through last loop formed.

Single Crochet (sc)

*Insert hook into the second chain from the hook (or the next stitch), yarn over hook and draw through a loop, yarn over hook (Figure 1), and draw it through both loops on hook (Figure 2). Repeat from * for the desired number of stitches.

Figure 1

Figure 2

Slip-Stitch Crochet (sl st)

*Insert hook into stitch, yarn over hook and draw a loop through both the stitch and the loop already on hook. Repeat from * for the desired number of stitches.

DECREASES

See also page 121.

Purl Two Together Through Back Loops (p2togtbl)

Bring right needle tip behind two stitches on left needle, enter through the back loop of the second stitch, then the first stitch, then purl them together.

EMBROIDERY

French Knot

Bring threaded needle out of knitted background from back to front, wrap yarn around needle one to three times, and use your thumb to hold the wraps in place while you insert needle into background a short distance from where it came out. Pull the needle through the wraps into the background.

I-CORD (ALSO CALLED KNIT-CORD)

Using two double-pointed needles, cast on the desired number of stitches (usually three to four). *Without turning the needle, slide stitches to other end of needle, pull the yarn around the back, and knit the stitches as usual. Repeat from * for desired length.

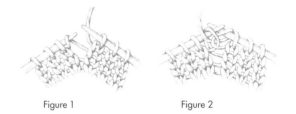

INCREASES

See also page 120.

Bar Increase (k1f&b)

Knit into a stitch but leave it on the left needle (Figure 1), then knit through the back loop of the same stitch (Figure 2) and slip the original stitch off the needle (Figure 3).

Figure 1

Figure 2

Figure 3

P1f&b

Purl into a stitch but leave it on the left needle (Figure 1), then purl through the back loop of the same stitch (Figure 2) and slip the original stitch off the needle.

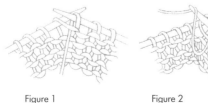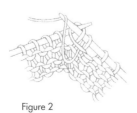

Figure 1

Figure 2

Purlwise Raised Increase (M1 pwise)

With left needle tip, lift the strand between the needles from back to front (Figure 1), then purl the lifted loop through the front (Figure 2).

Figure 1

Figure 2

YARNOVERS

Yarnover between two knit stitches

Wrap the working yarn around the needle from front to back and in position to knit the next stitch.

Yarnover after a knit before a purl

Wrap the working yarn around the needle from front to back then under the needle to the front again in position to purl the next stitch.

Yarnover between two purl sts

Wrap the working yarn around the needle from front to back, then under the needle to the front in position to purl the next stitch.

Yarnover after purl before knit

Wrap the working yarn around the needle from front to back and in position to knit the next stitch.

SIMPLE STYLE | ann budd

PICK UP AND KNIT

Pick Up and Knit Along Bind-Off or Cast-On Edge

With right side facing and working from right to left, insert the tip of the needle into the center of the stitch below the bind-off or cast-on edge (Figure 1), wrap yarn around needle, and pull through a loop (Figure 2). Pick up one stitch for every existing stitch.

Figure 1   Figure 2

Pick Up and Knit Along Shaped Edge

With right side facing and working from right to left, insert tip of needle between last and second-to-last stitches, wrap yarn around needle, and pull through a loop. Pick up and knit about three stitches for every four rows, adjusting as necessary so that picked-up edge lays flat.

Pick Up and Purl

With wrong side of work facing and working from right to left, *insert needle tip under selvedge stitch from the far side to the near side (Figure 1), wrap yarn around needle, and pull a loop through (Figure 2). Repeat from * for desired number of stitches.

Figure 1   Figure 2

SEAMS

Mattress Stitch

Place the pieces to be seamed on a table, right sides facing up. Begin at the lower edge and work upward as follows for your stitch pattern:

Stockinette Stitch with One-Stitch Seam Allowance

Insert threaded needle under one bar between the two edge stitches on one piece, then under the corresponding bar plus the bar above it on the other piece (Figure 1). *Pick up the next two bars on the first piece (Figure 2), then the next two bars on the other (Figure 3). Repeat from *, ending by picking up the last bar or pair of bars on the first piece.

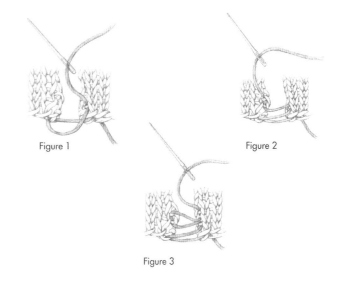

Figure 1   Figure 2

Figure 3

Stockinette Stitch with Half-Stitch Seam Allowance

To reduce bulk in the mattress stitch seam, work as for the one-stitch seam allowance but pick up the bars in the center of the edge stitches instead of between the last two stitches.

SHORT-ROWS

Short-Rows Knit Side

Work to turning point, slip next stitch
purlwise (Figure 1), bring the yarn to the
front, then slip the same stitch back to the
left needle (Figure 2), turn the work around
and bring the yarn in position for the next
stitch—one stitch has been wrapped
and the yarn is correctly positioned to
work the next stitch. When you come to
a wrapped stitch on a subsequent row,
hide the wrap by working it together with
the wrapped stitch as follows: Insert right
needle tip under the wrap (from the front
if wrapped stitch is a knit stitch; from the
back if wrapped stitch is a purl stitch;
Figure 3), then into the stitch on the
needle, and work the stitch and its wrap
together as a single stitch.

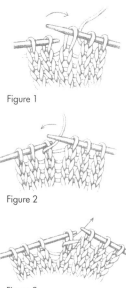

Figure 1

Figure 2

Figure 3

Short-Rows Purl Side

Work to the turning point, slip the next stitch
purlwise to the right needle, bring the yarn
to the back of the work (Figure 1), return the
slipped stitch to the left needle, bring the
yarn to the front between the needles (Figure
2), and turn the work so that the knit side is
facing—one stitch has been wrapped and
the yarn is correctly positioned to knit the
next stitch. To hide the wrap on a subsequent purl row, work to the wrapped stitch,
use the tip of the right needle to pick up
the wrap from the back, place it on the left
needle (Figure 3), then purl it together with
the wrapped stitch.

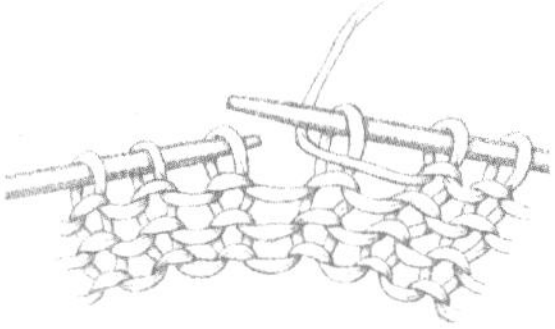

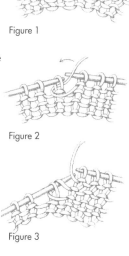

Figure 1

Figure 2

Figure 3

WEAVE IN LOOSE ENDS

The loose ends are the tails of yarn left hanging at the cast-on,
bind-off, and where new balls of yarn were added during the
knitting. You need to secure these ends on the wrong side of
the fabric so the knitting doesn't inadvertently ravel. Ideally, the
tails should be threaded on a tapestry needle and worked into
the seam allowances where there's no possibility of them being
visible on the right side of the work. Many expert knitters will only
change balls at the end of row. This can involve wasting a partial
row worth of yarn if there is enough yarn in the old ball to make
it partway across another row. If you do have tails hanging in the
middle of a row, thread the end on a tapestry needle and trace
the path of a row of stitches (Figure 2) or work along the diago-
nal, catching the back side (purl bumps) of the stitches (Figure 3).
To minimize weaving in ends, work the ends in as you knit as
described on page 115.

Figure 1

Figure 2

Pam Allen is creative director of Classic Elite Yarns and former editor in chief of *Interweave Knits*. She's the author of *Knitting for Dummies* (For Dummies, 2002) and *Scarf Style*, the first book in the Interweave Style series, and coauthor of *Wrap Style*, *Lace Style*, *Bag Style*, and *Color Style*.

Véronik Avery has been designing knitwear for a scant five years and is the author of *Knitting Classic Style: 35 Modern Designs Inspired by Fashion's Archives* (Stewart, Tabori and Chang, 2007). She lives in Montréal, Québec. Visit her website at veronikavery.com.

Ann Budd is the former senior editor of *Interweave Knits*. She is the author of *The Knitter's Handy Book* series and *Getting Started Knitting Socks*, and coauthor of *Wrap Style*, *Lace Style*, *Bag Style*, and *Color Style*.

Therese Chynoweth is an avid, mostly self-taught knitter. She particularly enjoys technical knitting and "engineering" her designs. Therese likes to find ways to incorporate finishing into the knitting phase so she can enjoy wearing sweaters as soon as the knitting is done. Therese lives in Vermont, where well-made wool sweaters are most appreciated.

Kat Coyle is an artist and knitter. Her book *Boho Baby Knits: Groovy Patterns for Cool Tots* (Potter Craft, 2007) is a collection of knitted clothes, accessories, and toys for the little ones. She chronicles her creativity and daily life on her blog at katcoyle.blogspot.com.

Cecily Glowik has a BFA with a concentration in painting, but knitting is her passion. She has been designing handknits for more than ten years and has had numerous designs featured in books, magazines, and Classic Elite Yarns collections.

Micki Hair is a fiber enthusiast who enjoys knitting, spinning, weaving, and designing. She lives with her husband and family of pets on their farm in the Midlands of South Carolina.

Alice Halbeisen has been knitting for six years and is new to designing. She lives in Lowell, Massachusetts, with a husband who earns enough to allow her to knit all day and two great teenagers (really!). When she does not have needles (or a crochet hook) in hand, she is squishing pests in her organic garden or burying her nose in a book.

Katie Himmelberg is the assistant editor of *Interweave Knits* and style editor of *Knitscene* magazines. In addition to knitting, she sews, makes jewelry, and cooks gourmet vegan meals.

Margaret Hubert started in the needle-arts business in 1963. Since then, she has written fifteen books, the latest of which is *Knits for Men: 20 Sweaters, Vests, and Accessories* (Creative Publishing International, 2008), and has had her designs published in many knitting and crochet magazines. She teaches knitting and crocheting workshops across the country.

Mags Kandis is a maker of stuff, designer of things, and author of *Folk Style* (Interweave, 2007), as well as seventeen pattern books for Mission Falls Yarns. Mags lives in Consecon, Ontario.

Deborah Newton of Providence, Rhode Island, designs all kinds of knitwear for magazines and yarn companies, as well fabrics for Seventh Avenue. She is the author of *Designing Knitwear* (Taunton, 1998).

Ruthie Nussbaum lives in New York City, where she's a reading teacher, knitting instructor, and burgeoning knitwear designer. See more of her work at ruthieknits.com.

Designer, author, pattern editor, and columnist, **Ann E. Smith** has been a contributor to the yarn industry for twenty-three years. She has a degree in home economics from Oklahoma University, with an emphasis in textiles and clothing construction, and has done graduate work in adult education at Kansas University.

Vicki Square is the author of several books, including *The Knitter's Companion*, *Folk Bags*, *Folk Hats*, and *Knit Kimono* from Interweave. At home in Fort Collins, Colorado, with her husband, Johnny, she and her newest Alaskan Malamute puppy, Samson, share a love for yarn and books, although Vicki prefers to knit the yarn rather than chew it.

JoLene Treace is a professional member of the Association of Knitwear Designers. JoLene has designs in a number of publications and also self publishes pattern leaflets through her business, Kristmen's Design Studio.

SOURCES FOR YARNS

BERROCO
PO Box 367
14 Elmdale Rd.
Uxbridge, MA 01569
berroco.com
In Canada: S. R. Kertzer Ltd.

BLACK WATER ABBEY YARNS
PO Box 470688
Aurora, CO 80047
blackwaterabbeyyarns.com

BLUE SKY ALPACAS INC.
PO Box 88
Cedar, MN 55011
blueskyalpacas.com

BROWN SHEEP COMPANY
100662 County Rd. 16
Mitchell, NE 69357
brownsheep.com

CLASSIC ELITE YARNS
122 Western Ave.
Lowell, MA 01851
classiceliteyarns.com

DALE OF NORWAY
4750 Shelburne Rd., Ste. 20
Shelburne, VT 05482
dale.no

DIAMOND YARN
9697 St. Laurent, Ste. 101
Montréal, QC
Canada H3L 2N1
and
155 Martin Ross, Unit 3
Toronto, ON
Canada M3J 2L9
diamondyarn.com

FIESTA YARNS
4583 Corrales Rd.
Corrales, NM 87048
fiestayarns.com

KNITTING FEVER INC./SIRDAR
PO Box 336
315 Bayview Ave.
Amityville, NY 11701
knittingfever.com
In Canada: Diamond Yarn

LALANA WOOLS
136-C Paseo del Pueblo Norte
Taos, NM 87571
lalanawools.com

LION BRAND YARN
135 Kero Rd.
Carlstadt, NJ 07072
lionbrand.com

LOUET NORTH AMERICA
808 Commerce Park Dr.
Ogdensburg, NY 13669
louet.com
In Canada: 3425 Hands Rd.
Prescott, ON K0E 1T0

MUENCH YARNS INC./GGH
1323 Scott St.
Petaluma, CA 94954-1135
muenchyarns.com
In Canada: Oberlyn Yarns

OBERLYN YARNS
5640 Rue Valcourt
Brossard, QC
Canada J4W 1C5
oberlyn.ca

S.R. KERTZER LTD.
6060 Burnside Ct., Unit 2
Mississauga, ON
Canada L5T 2T5
kertzer.com

SKACEL/SCHOELLER + STAHL
PO Box 88110
Seattle, WA 98138
skacelknitting.com

**TAHKI/STACY CHARLES INC./
FILATURA DI CROSA**
70–30 80th St., Bldg. 36
Ridgewood, NY 11385
tahkistacycharles.com
In Canada: Diamond Yarn

WESTMINSTER FIBERS/NASHUA/ROWAN
165 Ledge St.
Nashua, NH 03060
westminsterfibers.com
In Canada: Diamond Yarn